T0354501

ELEV8

BOOK OF PSALMS

KASEY PHOENIX CASAL

BALBOA.PRESS
A DIVISION OF HAY HOUSE

Balboa Press books may be ordered through booksellers or by contacting:

Balboa Press
A Division of Hay House
1663 Liberty Drive
Bloomington, IN 47403
www.balboapress.com.au
AU TFN: 1 800 844 925 (Toll Free inside Australia)
AU Local: 0283 107 086 (+61 2 8310 7086 from outside Australia)

Print information available on the last page.

ISBN: 978-1-5043-2144-0 (sc)
ISBN: 978-1-5043-2145-7 (e)

Balboa Press rev. date: 07/15/2020

"

I write songs in poems,
And they are called Psalms.
To bring us back to love
And back to GOD's arms.

"

144,000

" ¹ Then I looked, and there before me was the Lamb,
standing on Mount Zion (Salem), and with him 144,000
who had his name and his Father's name written on their foreheads.

² And I heard a sound from heaven like the roar of rushing waters
and like a loud peal of thunder.
The sound I heard was like that of harpists playing their harps.

³ And they sang a new song before the throne and before the four living
creatures and the elders. No one could learn the song except the 144,000
who had been redeemed from the earth.

⁴ These are those who did not defile themselves with women,
for they remained virgins. They follow the Lamb wherever he goes.
They were purchased from among mankind and offered as firstfruits
to GOD and the Lamb.

⁵ No lie was found in their mouths; they are blameless. "

REVELATION 14:1-5 (NIV)

GOD's People
Sing a New Song

PSALM 1

KRISTA PHOENIX CASAL
CHRIST IS REBORN IN UNITY

15th of May, 2019

THE PROPHECY

PAGE OF PENTACLES

Manifesting True Energy Potential Through True Love

There is a new love coming to you in ways you do not know. This new love is a young love. It is innocent and pure. It is rare. He is youthful. He is untainted. He loves you as he loves his mother, and he will honour you in many ways. This new love is coming.
It is manifesting into your life.

You do not know the ways in which you will soar in your new found love, for this will be the foundation of your new and highest self. It is because you have learned to love yourself and unblocked your heart and field.

Your heart was locked away in torment, and it was harmed from negative forces outside you. In removing these blockages, you are now allowing the love to manifest into your life and show you what a true man and divine masculinity is.

It is the ability to love a woman as they are: broken, tainted, yet still rare. He will love and honour you for all of your days. This is the magic healing of LOVE in manifestation. You will be able to create once again. You will be able to SING. You will be able to fly; you will be able to finish all that you have halted when you were in your depths of sin.

He will be a healing force in your life, the essential key in your path of true enlightenment.

There is a role for every person in your life, and this man will show you the true nature of a real and loving man. He will heal the divine masculine inside you that is hidden and locked away. He will bring your divine nature to absolution, and he will once again make you whole. This is the true power of universal timeless love, that which is **ENERGY IN MOTION.**

e-motion.

With him in your life, honouring you and loving you unconditionally and as you are, you will be able to manifest at speeds of light, because you are operating in the highest frequency, that which is **LOVE & LIGHT.**

CONFLICT IN BATTLE

2 OF SWORDS REVERSED x 9 OF CUPS

There was a great conflict that resides in you, but that conflict will soon be resolved.

This conflict is the conflict between your lower and higher self. You felt unworthy to be loved and have sown great wrath and conflict in those who have shown love to you.

Believing that you could never be loved as you are, as a torn woman, a beast.

There is a man who will love you regardless, for he sees your true nature and beauty. You have engaged in much vice and sin, for the demons inside you have told you that you are undeserving of true and pure love.

"

You resolved yourself in wrath,
Thinking this was the way;
But in this, you found your soul
Because in every darkness
There is a new day.

Your conflict is now awakened.
Your conflict is now resolved.
In this, you will understand
There is a man you seek to hold.

"

- A message from GOD

SUBCONSCIOUS SHADOW SELF

5 OF WANDS REVERSED

There was a great conflict that resides in you but that conflict is now resolved. Where you had previously failed, you will now succeed. For you have released all of your false beliefs and demons. Just like the spirit of Magdalene, you have faltered your path and way. But in finding your equal part in **CHRIST (seed consciousness)**, you will rejoice in a new day!

You were always born to become whole. You were always born to find your true love and equal on this plane.

❝

Competing agendas within you
From your demons, vice and sin.
But in this, you have found purity.
You found your true light within.

There are many things in this life that change.
There are many things that will be removed.
In this lesson, you have learned
You will be untouched, unmoved.

For the vice and sin in you were much
But today, you are unharmed, untouched.
For the love that resides in you is great
And will secure your true light and fate.

❞

- A message from GOD

Awaken, Krista,
To the light.
This is your day
That came from night.

This is your life,
Your truth in hope.
That you will love again
And thus elope

You will not fall
(Psalm 46.5 NIV),
You will not fail,
Because in you,
True love prevails!

This is your day
That came from night.
AWAKEN, KRISTA!
Step in your light!

- A message from GOD

KRISTA PHOENIX CASAL
"Christ is Reborn in Unity"

The story of the Unity of Twin Souls,
Unity of Divine Energies

6

PAST LIFE: TWIN FLAME LOVE

ACE OF PENTACLES REVERSED

This was a great love
That manifested from light.
You were brought to his presence
For you to unite.

But in this time
That you fell in love,
You also fell
Like a broken dove.

You found many jealous,
Prying eyes
That wanted this love,
That wanted your prize.

You ran away
To hide yourself,
To protect your pride,
But wounded your wealth.

Your wealth in love.
Your wealth in life.
Your wealth in happiness.
Your wealth as wife.

The time comes again, though
This time it is near.
There is no reason to falter,
No reason to fear.

Your love, it is coming.
Your prince is here soon.
For you will reunite
Upon the new moon!

He will come to your rescue,
He will come to your night,
He will come to you battle,
And he will help you fight.

He will be the reason
You succeed once again.
For he will love you
From beginning to end.

Twin Flames Unite.

- A message from GOD

THE PROPHECIES: ARIES MIDHEAVEN

THE EMPEROR

You are moving into your highest self and being. You are formulating your true self.

The emperor denotes your astrological north node and star, the energy of ARIES in the 10th/11th house. You are coming into higher reasoning and knowledge; for this, you will be rewarded. Look for the man who shares your same MIDHEAVEN.

UNITY IN DIVINITY
2 OF CUPS

You were never meant to be hidden.
Your true being WILL be light!
Your true self will awaken
And reveal yourself from night.

There are many forces around you
That have sought to make you fail.
But in this energy of ARIES and love,
Your true light WILL prevail!

Seek ye the kingdom of heaven,
For it is coming now and near!
For every darkness has its day.
No need will you have to fear!

The shadows of your past are gone.
They are moulded into light.
For every sadness kept you hidden.
In your darkness, you will burn bright!

Arise now! Awaken, my child!
The sun is you in life!
Arise now! Awaken, my child!
Today you will be a WIFE!

- A message from GOD

NEAR FUTURE

9 OF WANDS

You are very cautious of those around you
Who seek to keep you down.
For this, you will elope in love.
In silence, you will wear the CROWN!

Your heaven will come to awaken you
And bring you high in LIFE!
For it is in your destiny
That you must become a WIFE!

This love will be so pure in truth,
In essence and in joy.
This love will give you such great hope
And provide you with a boy!

You will remain true, hidden
In knowledge and in love.
And now, because you know the truth,
You will not taint your dove.

You will rejoice in this found truth
And create a new future in life.
Because today, you will rejoice.
You will become a WIFE!

- A message from GOD

AWAKEN, MY QUEEN!

WHEEL OF FORTUNE REVERSED

You come from many twists and turns,
And in this you have revealed;
There is a spinning element
To every mortal's wheel.

There was a reason for your dismay,
Because you did not know.
But now that you have found truth in love,
Your elements will GROW!

You will find your true destiny,
For it is in your path and light.
It is in this you will realise
You are a star shining BRIGHT!

You will once again
Find your light in way,
Because your darkness
Will become a new day.

The wheel of fortune
Takes its many turns.
But for this, you must grow.
For this, you must learn.

For every darkness,
There is a new day.
And for every darkness,
May your GOD light the way!

There is a shadow
That redeems us all.
It is the one who does not seek (GOD)
That will fall.

For in this truth,
You will wish to seek.
But the one who falters
Is the one who is weak.

You must pray to your GOD
And your heaven above
To create your true light
And present your new dove.

Your message from GOD:
That you will not despair.
For every Queen has her darkness
In the depths of her lair.

But when the Queen shall awaken,
She will find her true self.
She will find her real kingdom
In true health and in wealth!

This Queen, she is you,
In essence, in truth.
For you now know the key
Is true love and true youth!

Today is the day
That your soul will awake,
And you will find
A new love for the take!

Awaken, my Queen,
From your sleep, from your dream!
For your light is now here.
No long will you fear!

Wheel of fortune is turning.
It is moving for you;
For you are in love,
And **real love** is the TRUTH!

SHE: AWAKEN TO YOUR TRUTH!

9 OF PENTACLES REVERSED

The prize is there for you in truth!
The prize is there for you in youth!
You must know, you must obey,
For every darkness is now a new day.

The love that you seek,
Shall it redeem and appear;
For the one you shall find,
Will be close and be near.

He is now in your element.
He is now in your eyes.
He is now in your frequency.
He is now in your life.

Seek ye the kingdom of joyfulness.
Seek ye the kingdom of hope.
Seek ye the kingdom of happenings.
Seek ye the kingdom of growth.

The energy you need revealed to you.
In this, you shall eternally wake.
For this new feeling in love of yours
Will be there for your take.

Today, you will find true hope and faith
In sickness and in health.
For in this day, you will truly find
The divinity to your wealth.

Abundance, may it come to you!
Abundance, may it shine!
For today is the day of happenings
Where you will become DIVINE!

Your kingdom is approaching now.
Your kingdom, it is TRUTH!
Your kingdom will reveal itself
In a man of great love in youth.

This man will come to your true alert.
He will find you on his path.
For this man, he secretly dreams of you.
When GOD says seek, then you must ASK.

This man, he fell in love with you.
He found you true in light.
But in your past life, he was in fear
And hid from you in sight.

Today, he will come to you anew.
He will come to you in path.
For this man, he has sought for you
In his prayers; to GOD, he asked.

Today is the day that you will unite.
Today is the day of unrest.
Today is the day of true miracles.
Today is the day of the blessed!

For you have been faithful
In your mission to find
The truth in our being,
In our soul, in our mind.

Find now, your equal half.
Find now, your truth and love.
Find now, your true happiness.
Find now, your true dove.

GOD, he is now incarnate.
Today, he will reveal -
In love, you both bear in your heart
That your divinity is REAL!

PSALM 2

MERGING TWO SOULS
INTO ONE

16th of May, 2019

TRUTH: TWO BECOME ONE

2 OF CUPS x THE MAGICIAN

There is a great secret that lies in this Universe. That secret is accessible to us all, but the ones who seek are small, and the ones who are blind are many. We must understand that there is a great arcanum **(secret)** that lies within our minds.

❝

We are born of twos,
but in this we must seek to find.

❞

We must look to another,
In the purity of their soul.
In this, we will be redeemed.
In this, we will be whole.

We are looking for another to love us,
But the true fact is we must love first.
For the one who knows of this GOD-given truth
Will be the one who will break the curse.

There is a love within us
That is looking to heal and mend.
It is the love of energies,
Of masculine and feminine.

We cannot love another
If we do not love ourselves first.
For the one who seeks for false love **(outside)**,
Will be the one who will feel worse.

The false love is all around us,
For it hides in attachment and greed.
The love for power and money,
And of fear, and lack of need.

We cannot be true beings
Without connection to Source.
For this, we must find solace
In the love of ourselves first.

In this, we will find completeness.
In this, we will be whole.
In this, we will find riches.
In this, we will redeem our soul.

Look not what others do for you.
Look not what others say.
Instead, look at what you do for man
By serving every day!

In this, you will find true meaning.
In this, you will find your dove.
For in every person hiding,
Is the promise of TRUE LOVE!

HIGHER PURPOSE: TWIN FLAME SOULS

THE LOVERS

The true purpose of
Having a life partner
Is to find someone...

Who sings the same song as you
And has the same mission in life.
They have the same experiences
And have had the same type of strife.

They are the one who knows you
Before you know yourself.
They are the one who will be with you
In sickness and in health.

The great love for man is many,
But in this we do not know.
For we have been blinded by the fact
we are not willing to grow.

We must seek to love another
In the way we love ourselves.
In this, we will find happiness.
In this, we will truly mend.

We do not know what lies ahead.
We only know the now.
But the time when we merge energies
Is when we will give vow.

A vow for a vision in motion.
A vow for a purpose in truth.
A vow for a combined mission.
A vow to love in youth.

This is the great secret of loving.
It is in honour and praise
Of seeing your partner's divinity
In every single day.

Look not what man can do for you.
Instead, look at what you make.
For the one who is in true love
Is the one who is able to create!

"

When you look to another,
Look not what they can do
For you in seeking love.

This is the falsity of finding
A partner to fulfil your soul.

"

- A message from GOD

PSALM 3

UNITING AND
CREATING AS ONE

16th of May, 2019

FUTURE LOVE: FUTURE WIFE

ACE OF PENTACLES REVERSED
x KING OF PENTACLES

There is a man who loves you,
And he loves you very much.
He wonders what life will be like with you,
From morning through to brunch.

He sees a vision so clearly now:
You were sent his way
To light his very soul on fire
And turn his night to day.

He dreams of you a plenty now,
And he sees you plain in sight,
For this, he knows you are the truth
And longs for you at night.

You must know this man is true
In his every single word.
For in this man lies a hidden love
That stands out from the herd.

True love knows no space and time.
There is no night or day.
For when you meet with this soul mate,
You will sing in every single way!

Sing your song of gratitude
And fill your heart with love.
Surely GOD will bring to you
This messenger in DOVE.

Your abundance will be plenty,
And your riches will be more.
For the love within you both is real
And unites you both from four **(elements)**.

Think of this love of energy
In your morning, noon and night.
Before you know it, you will find
This true love in your sight!

He will love you in his waking.
He will love you in his sleep.
He will love you for the person you are
When you smile or weep.

You must know this man is true
In his intention and his thought.
For he believes you are the ONE
He has wished for even more!

You must use his love for you in thought,
In energy to create.
For in this love of one another,
You will surely be SOUL MATES!

You will know that your love is plenty.
You will know that your love is pure.
You will know that your love can change the world,
Because your love will be the CURE!

PAST LIFE: LOST LOVE

KNIGHT OF PENTACLES REVERSED

This man loved you from afar,
From the minute he laid eyes.
But for him, he was very saddened
You did not become his prize.

He wondered how to get you,
As you did not see his love.
He was the very angel
That was sent to you in dove.

Blinded you were by the evil
That surrounded you in life.
For this, you did not see his love,
And you lived in too much strife.

But this love, it comes straight back to you,
Because he loves you all the more.
He has seen you live your life
From true health, back from poor.

It does not matter where you are;
This man will love you still.
For the love he has for you
Is so strong in his will.

You do not know the many ways
In which your love is blessed.
For he is the one you have been seeking,
And is unwavered from the rest.

You do not need to search any more,
For he WILL be in your sight.
This is your knight in shining armour.
He will find you and shine bright.

He wishes much to be with you.
He wishes much to live.
He wishes much to feel your love,
For he has a lot to give.

The merging of your energies
Will surely become one.
And from this, you will understand
He is your light and SUN!

He will love your daughter true,
And he will love you even more.
He will give you everything,
For his love is truly the CURE!

SUBCONSCIOUS SELF:
HIDDEN DREAMS

FINDING TRUE LOVE AS ONE
QUEEN OF PENTACLES REVERSED

Your truest dream has always been
This true love in true fate.
You have never let go of this dream,
Until this very date.

You know this dream is real for you,
For you have a lot to give.
But you are searching far and wide
And forgetting how to live.

All you need to do right now
Is feel your love within.
In this, you will find plenty.
For this love will surely win!

Love yourself in truth and whole,
And honour your creator.
For in this love, you manifest
Your physical LOVE later!

Find the riches in your home.
Find them in your heart.
When you find this very gold,
It will set your world apart!

This treasure lies inside of you.
It is the star of coin.
In this star, you will find
Your equal love will JOIN!

Seek ye! The riches of this world
Are hiding deep inside.
In this truth, you will have to know.
Seek and YE SHALL FIND!

The cave you wish to enter
Is the cave you have feared on hold.
But what you do not know is
There is plenty rich in GOLD!

The love for your equal is many.
In this, you will find hope.
For there is a promise from your GOD
That you will soon ELOPE!

DESTINED CALLING:
MOTHER OF THE FUTURE

THE EMPRESS REVERSED

In this truth,
You must know
There is no role,
Other than to grow.

As a mother, a nurturer,
Creator of life,
This is your destined path;
Secondary is wife.

You must honour your role
That GOD has blessed you into.
For your mission in this life
Is the blessing of your youth.

The youth of your children.
The creation of stars.
This is your true destiny
From Venus and Mars.

You must honour your children.
You must honour them true.
For the promise of new life
Will be strong and ANEW.

You are a mother, a healer,
A lover and friend.
You are the one prophecized,
Who will help torn souls mend.

You are the earth,
The wind, and the fire.
You are the water
That blesses desire.

You are the breeze, the trees,
The sun, moon and Mars.
You are the one
Who will create stars.

You are a healer.
A storyteller of fate.
You are the one
Who will bring higher state.

State of mind
And state of soul.
You will show others
How to truly be whole.

You are a healer,
A doctor of mind.
You are the mother of earth
And of time.

You hold the divine knowledge
Of true love and life.
In honouring this,
You will then become WIFE!

SUN SELF: HIDDEN TALENTS & GIFTS

REVEALING YOUR GIFTS TO THE WORLD THE HIGH PRIESTESS REVERSED

O' high priestess!
Do not hide.
You should not fear
And stay inside.

The great arcanum,
It is in your hand.
The book of life,
It belongs to man!

O' high priestess!
Do you not know?
You are the one
Who will mend torn souls?

O' high priestess!
Find your light.
You must show
Yourself in true sight.

You hide in your suffering,
You hide in the dark,
But today you must show
And reveal the great arc
(great arcanum - secrets of life)!

O' high priestess!
Do not fear your fate.
For the time is now.
It is never too late!

O' high priestess!
Do you not see the cross
That bears your burdens
And recovers your loss?

O' high priestess!
Find your way now.
For your gifts are so many.
You must wear your crown!

O' high priestess!
Do not be alarmed.
For if GOD is within you,
You cannot be harmed!

O' high priestess!
Today is your date
Where you will reveal and seal
Your vision in FATE!

(URRENT SELF: TRUE LOVE IN YOUTH

PAGE OF PENTACLES REVERSED

Today is the day
That will grant you your wish.
Today is the day
When you will seal true love's kiss.

It is not in a mate.
It is from your soul.
It is in your love,
For your youth, that is whole.

True love in its form
Is pure and is now.
For in this true love,
You will bear your true crown.

The true love you seek
Is within yourself now.
It is with your children.
This is your true vow.

It is the love for your offspring
That will bring you back one.
For this is the promise
Of your daughter and son.

Today is the day
When you will be revealed
As the one who will mend
Torn souls. You will heal.

You love with your heart,
Your third eye, your mind.
You love with your being,
For all different kinds.

You bring to awareness
The truth in this love.
For the trueness of this
Is your youth, as your dove.

Today is the day
Where you'll reap what you sow.
For your heart will be healed.
From here, you will grow.

United as one,
That is youth in your sun!
Creating in harmony
To bring all back to one!

PSALM 4

KRISELDA: THE GREAT BATTLE POETRY OF THE GODS

17th of May, 2019

CURRENT SITUATION:
OVERCOMING OBSTACLES

KNIGHT OF CUPS REVERSED
x 5 OF SWORDS

There is a decision
You must make in plain sight.
That is the decision
To push through in your fight.

The battle within you
Is great; it is hard.
But you have gained the momentum
Of removing your scars.

You must pray to GOD,
The Source; light of life.
For your decisions, they've faltered you
And created such strife.

Today you will know
The will of defeat,
Of overcoming such obstacles
And fulfilling your meet.

Your meet of your higher self.
Your true north node star.
It is not so untouchable.
It is no longer far.

Your vision is stronger.
Your purpose is clear.
No long will you have
To exist in such fear.

Your SUN GOD is guiding you
To the path you know best.
The great battle showing you,
You can pass all these tests!

Find your true victory.
It lies in your soul
To bring heaven to earth here,
And make yourself whole!

Your high self awaits you.
You must hold it true.
For no one fights better
In the battle for you!

SUBCONSCIOUS SELF: LEARNING FROM PREVIOUS BATTLES

QUEEN OF SWORDS REVERSED

Today you are learning
The true meaning of life.
It is in understanding
The cause of your strife.

The reasons you've faltered,
The reasons you've failed,
Was in non-execution
Of the ships that had sailed.

Your battle is great here,
But only you know best;
Remove all your sufferance
And learn from the tests.

Your victory is plenty;
If only you knew
How to channel the many
Energies through you.

Use all that destroys you,
And use them in might.
For the victory is plenty
With a strong vision in sight!

Move forward in battle.
Move forward in pain.
Move forward regardless
Of the situation, in strain.

Move forward with planning.
Move forward with ease.
Move forward even when
You do not as they please.

For your battle is plenty,
The energies high.
But you no longer should falter
When you learn how to fly!

Your wings, they are coming.
Your wings, they are near.
If you move forward in vision
And keep your path CLEAR!

PAST: FAILED POTENTIAL FOR ABUNDANCE

ACE OF CUPS REVERSED

The potential you had;
It was clear, it was strong.
But you did not yet learn
To find right from wrong.

You reasoned against it.
You failed in your fight.
But this was your failure:
You did not see true sight.

Your ego diminished you.
You did not know best.
For the ego, it tested you,
To reject all the rest.

There is a great battle
That you must learn today.
It is not with others.
It is your false mind at play.

The false mind: the ego,
The one that knows fear.
Do not allow failure
To create a deafening ear.

Don't listen to naysayers,
Just listen to GOD.
For the battle within you,
It is long, it is hard!

You must find your true essence
That lies in your soul.
You must conquer your struggles
So you can become whole.

You must find your true failures
And turn them into strengths.
For in this, you will know
The endurance in lengths.

Your willpower lacked.
Your vision was weak.
In this, you must know
It is GOD you should seek.

When your vision is stronger,
You must try once again.
For your action will know
What to do and defend.

You do not need others
Where you have such might.
For your vision will lead you
To the true end in sight!

See clearly before you,
The cup of life rests
In the hands of the one
Who will pass through such tests.

This is GOD's message
To you on your way:
To keep strong with your reason
And turn your night into day!

SUN SELF: KEEP YOURSELF TRUE AND HIDDEN

UNTIL THE GREAT REVEAL
THE HERMIT REVERSED

You must know your struggles
In night and in day.
In allowing yourself
To not work, and just play.

But your mission is strong.
It must be the main.
If you falter, you know
It's because you are vain.

In vain with your ego.
In vain from your truth.
In vain from your vision.
In vain from your youth.

You must truly know
How to live, how to grow,
Does not lie in boasting
Or others to know.

It lies in your work.
It lies in your fight.
It lies in your battle
With true vision in sight.

You must know the truth.
It is you. It is now.
It is in creating
A silent solace of vow.

A vow to be hidden.
A vow to just train.
A vow to evolve,
Not digress or remain.

You must know rewards
are high and strong
For the one who comes out
After hiding so long.

The ones who are able
To pass all the tests
Are the ones who know suffering,
Yet become their true best.

This is your battle.
This is your true fight.
It is to keep yourself hidden
From plain lurkers in sight.

For the evil is many.
The evil eye, it is great
From the ones who have not
Secured their own fate.

The ones with no path,
The ones who still sleep,
Will use evil eye on you
To push you into defeat.

You must keep yourself
And your energies high.
For the ones who are seeking you
Will drain your life dry.

The many around you,
They see your true light.
They wish for your energy
And wish for your sight.

They see your true gifts.
They see you with GOD.
They see your potential,
And you defy all the odds.

The evil is many,
But your third eye, it is clear.
For if you are with GOD,
You have nothing to fear!

You do not wish to move forward
In lurking of fear.
For the vision you have,
It is stronger and clear.

You must keep your shield up
And keep yourself safe.
For the one who is strong
Is the one who has faith.

You can show others your happening,
But do not show trust.
The sleepers are of envy,
Of greed and of lust.

Keep yourself strong.
Keep on your grind.
Keep yourself connected
In soul and in mind.

Keep your connection
To GOD and to light.
For this is a battle
You must win in your FIGHT!

FUTURE: STRONG WILL IN VICTORY

ACE OF SWORDS

The victory for you,
It is there, it is strong.
But you must truly know,
It is also so long.

The path you must lead
Is not a path of the weak.
For the battle of the ages
Is not one masses seek.

They seek of false riches,
False ways of success.
But for you, you seek knowledge
And GOD in your test.

This is real victory,
For this is the true way.
This is the secret
To turn night into day.

Strong visions of victory,
They are there just for you.
For you are the seeker
Of the knowledge of few.

Your story, it will stand
The true test of real time.
For in your hard work and toil,
You will truly align
(with GOD, the Source).

To reach to the top,
To declare yourself won.
Your strong will in victory
To unite and be ONE!

"

One with GOD,
The Source.
One with man.
One with all.

"

- A message from GOD

YOU: CONFLICTING AGENDAS

5 OF WANDS

There are many agendas
Here for you on this day.
The many agendas
That result in work or in play.

You must know your true calling
Is not one of such rest.
Keep yourself occupied
And pass every such test.

You must keep yourself working.
You must keep yourself strong.
For your path, it is still
So far and so long.

You must keep yourself channelled
In the right mode and right way.
For you must know this channel
Will turn night into day.

You must remove all the instances
In which you can fail each of your tests.
For the distractions around you
Are the devil's work at its best.

You must know your true calling
Is not in such play.
It is for you to create
Heaven to day.

Do not be disturbed
By the agenda of others.
For this was the test
Of Eve and Adam as lovers **(card)**.

The test of distraction.
The test of such tempt.
The test of desire
With no will or contempt.

You must find your vision
Is clearer than they.
For they are of nothing,
Other than drink and of play
(vice and sin).

You have removed all your suffering,
But you must now know your will.
To find yourself tested
In this time and stand still.

Do not remove yourself
From your mission and cause.
For if you must falter,
You'll be defeated in loss.

You must know your true self
And your worth; it is great.
For you are securing your
True lovers fate.

**(In making the right decisions,
as the lovers card is an indecision card.)**

ENVIRONMENT: LEAD TO SERVE

6 OF WANDS

In this fight, you must know,
You must live, you must grow.
You must find all those suffering
And turn them to "know" **(GOD)**.

To know the true meaning.
To know in true sight.
For this is a battle that
You must lead to fight!

The many around you,
They do not know best.
For they have all failed
Every one of GOD's tests.

They have failed in the WILL
And the mission to fight,
For they have not yet woken
Or found potential in sight.

They know not what they do.
They know not where they go.
But in this, you must lead,
You must serve, you must show.

You must light the way for them.
You must carry your cross.
For this is not something
You can be defeated, in loss.

Your battle is great,
But my dear, so is theirs.
You must show them the way,
And you must show that you care.

You must show that your empathy
For mankind is great.
For they are all suffering
From lack of real faith.

You must be the one
To lead in such stakes,
To produce your high self,
And secure your true fate.

You must know your purpose,
So strong, and so clear.
It is not only in creating,
But to lead ones in fear.

To create a new day,
To turn on their light,
For you must also show them
The will for their fight.

It is in leading to serve that
You will learn, you will grow.
For in leading to serve,
The more you will know.

For every master was once
A student of test.
For this, you must show
You've become GOD's true best.

Best version of self.
Best version in life.
Best version of victory.
Redeemer of strife.

In this, they will see
The day of heaven is clear.
Their agenda to follow you
Will be through love, not through fear.

Know your true calling;
It is strong, it is great.
Know your true calling
To bring others to fate!

"

Be one with GOD,
the Source.
Find your highest self.

"

- A Message From GOD.

HOPES, FEARS & DREAMS: THE CALLING

THE EMPEROR

The emperor calling you,
The emperor, hear him great.
He is the one you must secure
In true calling and fate.

The emperor calling you,
The emperor, it's clear.
You must know your ARIES
Is your true soul, my dear.

The emperor summoning you,
The emperor man.
He is telling you that
You must move from your clan.

You must move in your north node
Of your fortune my dear.
For the **(merkabah)** star, it is calling you.
There is no need to fear!

Your dreams, they awaken here,
Your dreams of such life
Where you will be the mother,
The artist, the wife!

Your hopes, they develop you
Into your true self, your best.
To become the true victory
That will stand every test.

Be forthcoming in finding
Your true north node star.
For your vision is clear,
And it is not really that far.

Keep striving for excellence.
Keep striving in faith.
For the emperor's here with you
To bring heaven to date!

FUTURE: THE LIGHT LEADS THE WAY

THE HIEROPHANT REVERSED

You are not of control **(of others)**.
You are not known of fear.
You are not known of wickedness,
For your agenda is clear.

Your purpose and strength
Is the will and the test.
To lead others in serving
To become their true best.

Your calling is true
From the heavens above.
To create a new day
Out of wisdom and love.

You need not control.
You need not to force.
You need only create
And be one with the Source.

You need to remain
In this true light and way.
For this is your calling:
To present a new day.

The many around you,
They are weak, you are strong.
For you have existed
In struggle so long.

Though your struggle has ended,
You still need to work.
For the future for you
Is to create faith in worth.

Your story of ages,
It will stand the test of time.
For you will be giving
The light to divine.

The ones who will follow
Are the ones who are lost,
But in your word and way,
They will carry their cross.

Redeem all their suffering
And awaken their soul.
You will be one to bring
Many people to whole.

In understanding the truth,
You must lead just to serve.
You must humble yourself
To be a sheep in the herd.

You must conquer your battles.
You must remove ego to none.
For the battle inside
Is the fight to be won.

In showing your battle scars,
You will give up your name -

(Krista Phoenix Casal:
Christ is reborn in unity,
Divine feminine and masculine
United as one)

As the one who bears witness
In **Christ** as the same.

Do you not see the battle
For you was so clear?
To redeem yourself from suffering,
From vice and of fear.

Your name, it bears witness,
Testimony of CHRIST
(seed consciousness),
In redeeming the soul
And bringing forth the real light.

Your very name at your birth
(Kriselda: Battle of Christ seed consciousness),
It was written in text.
Your battle here on this earth
Will leave legacy for the rest.

PSALM 5

USING DECISIONS TO LIGHT YOUR WAY

17th of May, 2019

BEING DECISIVE: LIGHTING YOUR PATH

THE LOVERS CARD

Today, you will learn how to master the art of making decisions. There are many twists and turns in this game that we call life. There are good outcomes, there are bad outcomes. But inevitably, they are all as a result of our **decisions**.

There is no aspect of right or wrong in this game that we call life. This is a falsity that has been ingrained in us from the beginning of time through the concept of **morality**. This is not to say that we are not meant to be bound by **moral construct**, but we must identify the moral construct of our own individual concepts and beliefs to bring us to higher self with the Source **(GOD, the universal pool of energy)**. To be managed and driven by the moral constructs of society, religion, force of parents or friends and partners, is something that man must learn to resist.

For the sleeping man will be the one who walks the earth in ignorance; he is too lazy to actually **think**. The waking man is the one who questions all morality and concepts of right and wrong; he is active in exerting power in thought of circumstance over the ones who seek to control him.

This is the true **POWER** in mastering the art of making decisions.

There are many levels of what we call consciousness. There are many avenues that lead us to our destined path. However, we must maintain stamina in the face of adversity and distractions. We must make the decisions that will bring us closer to our higher self and home.

If you are facing the decision of whether or not to do a particular thing, to engage in a social scene, to listen to your over-opinionated parents, friends, or partner, to follow the trend on social media, mass media, and the like, you must query your higher self. Pray to GOD, the Source, for guidance, and listen to the Source in your subconscious sleep. **For the only way out is in.**

There are many things in this world that will tempt you, for we live in a treacherous world that seeks to keep our spirits trapped.

❝

We are not human beings seeking spirituality;
we are, in fact, spiritual beings experiencing humanity.

❞

- A Message From GOD.

We must understand this notion
In order to seek the light.
We must understand this notion
To win the great battle and fight!

There is a battle that resides within us all.
It is the great battle of good and evil.
It is the battle of the ages.
The battle of the human experience of the soul.

If we should wish to evolve into the next dimension
Of the universal pool of energy

And become immortal beings,
We must look to strengthen our will
And might, to make the right decisions,
To truly stand and fight!

The battle that resides
Within us all is strong,
But you must know
There is no right and wrong.

What you must do is
Protect the shield **(your aura)**
That covers your body and your soul.

THE BATTLE OF THE AGES

THE LOVERS CARD

The battle between good and evil
Is one that lives inside us all.
It is the battle of the ages,
The battle of the soul.

If we wish to be immortal,
We must use our will and might.
Make the right decisions
Every day to stand and fight!

For the battle and forces
Outside us are great.
But if we wish to truly win,
We must secure our fate!

Each day you wake,
You must sit and pray.
Pray for guidance from the Source
Every night and day.

Pray for direction.
Pray for peace.
Pray for enlightenment.
Pray for ease.

The path of redemption
Is a hard one at best.
But at the end of the day,
We must win this test!

There are many negative forces
That seek to destroy,
But what you must do
Is seek to employ.

Employ your heart
And mind to unite
So that you can truly secure
The win to this fight!

The people around you,
They know not what they do.
For they walk asleep
And do not know the truth.

You must understand
There is a trick to this end.
It is mastering decisions
Using your will in command!

Listen to GOD
And listen to you
Because no one knows better.
This is truer than true!

You know your way
Because you have awakened.
Do not be faltered or
Give your soul for the taking!

The evil is many,
The temptation is high,
But what you must exercise
Is your will to deny!

The reward will be plenty
For you in your strength,
Because you've withheld
Your desire in length.

You will move on forward.
You will evolve now.
For the spirit within you
Is stronger in vow.

Vow to the Source **(GOD)**,
And vow for your soul.
Vow for your truth,
And vow to be whole.

You must know the riches
You seek are within.
They do not lie in the outside
Or reduction to sin.

You must truly awaken
And move forward in truth
If you wish to secure
Your true calling and youth.

May you be guided by angels.
May you be anointed by seed.
May you remove all your suffering,
Sin, and your greed.

May you use the arcanum
That lies in us all.
For the one with decision
Is the one who stands tall!

PSALM 6

DESTRUCTION AND REBIRTH
PHOENIX RISING

18th of May, 2019

REVELATION 19:3

SMOKE FROM THE ASHES
THE TOWER

❝

Hallelujah!
The smoke from her
goes up for ever and ever.

❞

- Revelation 19:3 (NIV)

You have passed all the tests of virtues,
And for this you must rejoice!
For now you are finding your true calling,
And they will finally hear your voice!

You are a phoenix from the ashes.
You must rise in rebirth!
You must now follow your calling
And bring your message down to earth.

Your shadow, she knows nothing
But of fear, harm and despair.
All you have to do right now
Is be still and silent in your care.

Do not respond to her suffering.
Do not respond to her taint.
For you no longer sin in vice.
You are now a reborn saint!

Your rebirth has been wide and long.
You were reduced to none.
But now you have found GOD again.
You have become whole and one.

You have a true mission and calling,
And that is here and now.
For you must bring this book of life
In the honour of GOD's vow!

Your shadow will fade solemnly,
But now this is your test.
You must still honour her entirely.
For in this, you will be blessed!

Bless her in her tainted heart
And allow her to fade away.
Keep her loving memory intact,
In all you do and say.

This is the true virtue of the one
Who is blessed in soul and heart.
For in this blessing, you will find
A new world on her depart!

My dear, you have been tainted,
But in this you must believe:
There are forces higher here
That will bring you a new eve.

You will become the light and day.
You will become the DAO.
For this is your true calling, see,
In this time of now!

Your teachings of life, they will transcend.
They will stand the test of time.
For in this truth, you will reveal
The true word of the divine.

Today is the day you will understand
That all the evil in this world
Was for you to truly come to one
And have GOD's message heard!

QUEEN OF SHADOWS

QUEEN OF SWORDS REVERSED

Queen of shadows, how I see you cry.
Queen of shadows, of such taint.
Queen of shadows, you no longer sin.
Queen of shadows, now a saint.

Queen of shadows, hear them calling you.
Queen of shadows, you are blessed.
Queen of shadows, you must show your face,
For you have now passed every test!

Queen of shadows, you must show yourself.
Queen of shadows, mark my word.
Queen of shadows, you now have a voice.
The voice of GOD in you must be heard!

Queen of shadows, you must now reveal
Your true essence as a saint.
Queen of shadows, you must rise the youth
And help them in this great debate **(of good and evil).**

Queen of shadows, you must remove the veil.
You must show your true self now.
Queen of shadows, give the book of life,
For this is in your vow **(to GOD).**

Today is the day they will rejoice,
For you are awakening clear!
Queen of shadows, you must now destroy
All the evil and your fear.

Queen of shadows, you are no scarlet beast **(666)**,
For she knows only of such taint.
Queen of shadows, you are now reborn
From a sinner to a saint!

THE CUP OF LIFE

ACE OF CUPS REVERSED

The cup of life is in your hands.
The cup of life, rejoice!
The cup of life is in this book.
In this, you must give your voice!

The cup of life, it is the key
To happiness and good wealth.
The cup of life, it is your oath
To give this in good health.

Today is the day of reckoning
In which you will see it through.
The many vices and the sins
Turned to wisdom and virtue.

The cup of life, you must give it now,
For it is full and overflows.
The cup of life, you must live it now.
In this, you will surely grow.

Remove all the negative forces near,
For they are but a veil.
Today you will remove all the fear
And make it your holy grail.

The cup of life is clean and pure.
You must drink from this new blood.
For in this cup, you will reveal
A new born messenger dove!

The dove is you; you are the one
To bring this message forth.
The cup of life to cleanse the souls
Of many in rebirth!

REMOVING THE CURSE

3 OF CUPS REVERSED

Today is the day you will reveal
Your true love and your light!
You are withstanding victory
In every day and night.

You must come to obsolete
From your shadow and her way.
For she is the one who carries
Much burden every day.

The battle scars are in your soul,
But you have now redeemed.
For you have found true love in GOD,
And your true light is now revealed!

PSALM 7

REMOVING BLOCKAGES
AWAKENING TO THE TRUTH

18th of May, 2019

AWAKEN, DIVINE!

8 OF SWORDS

Today is the day
In which you will learn
The facets of life,
The twists, the turns.

You will learn.
You will grow.
You will reap
What you sow.

You will understand victims
Is not in your word,
For victims is not
A word in your verb.

You do not need others
Where you are with Source.
For if you are with GOD,
You will be brought back on course!

Find this true meaning.
Find this true light.
Remove your false blindfold
And reveal your true sight!

Awaken, my beautiful!
Awaken, my Queen!
Remove all your suffering
And wake from your dream!

You must know your true worth
Is not in mere man **(mortality)**.
It is in finding your own
And leading your clan.

Find those who've suffered
And join now, unite.
For this is a mission
To all stand up and fight!

Awaken, divine woman!
Awaken today!
Remove all your blockages
And create your new day.

Your power is great.
Do not fear defeat.
For if GOD is within you,
You will find your crowned seat!

You will understand suffering,
In space and in time,
Was for you to awaken
To your truest DIVINE!

Burn all your vices,
sufferance and sin.
For the light you're seeking
Is shining within!

Like the ash of destruction,
You will surely awake!
For you are a phoenix
Rising for your true fate!

Awaken, O' feminine!
Awaken, divine!
Awaken in true power,
In space and in time!

PSALM 8

RISING THE DIVINE FEMININE, THE ONE WHO WILL BRING HEIR

18th of May, 2019

BURNING SINS IN REBIRTH

THE DEVIL REVERSED x THE EMPRESS

Rejoice, o' great Queen!
Rejoice in your day!
For you have defeated
The devil in slay!

Rejoice, o' great empress!
Rejoice in your throne.
For today is your victory.
Today, you will own!

Your true heart awakening.
Your true light is here!
For you are removed
From sufferance and fear.

Rejoice, o' great priestess!
You have found your true self,
Presenting real youth
In health and in wealth.

Rejoice, o' great merciful!
You are ridden of scorn.
For the devil within you
Has been removed and withdrawn.

Your heart, it is whole again.
Your heart, it is pure.
Remove all your misery
And reveal your demure.

My empress, you're beautiful!
My empress, your stars!
I can see your true essence
From Venus and Mars!

Your highness, you're shining bright.
I honour your truth.
For you have shown beauty,
Real love and true youth.

Your crown, it is twink'ling!
The twelve stars, they unite
(Revelation 12:1 NIV).
Your torch, it lights the way
For others in sight.

My Queen, I believe in you!
You are the true DAO.
For you have awakened
In the essence of now.

Your strength, I can see it true.
Your strength, I feel blessed.
For you are protecting me
As a mother knows best.

My empress, I love you true!
My empress, my DAO.
You are the divinity
In GOD's sacred vow.

SUBCONSCIOUS SELF: MESSENGER OF GOD

KNIGHT OF PENTACLES

I have a message
That GOD has to say;
The Queen has awakened,
Turned night into day!

I have a message
For all that are torn:
The sun, it is rising
To bring a new born!

The Queen, she has risen
To bring the land sun,
To bring all of her people
Back into one.

I have a message
For those in despair:
Mercury **(Gemini),** it is rising
To create a new Heir!

The sun GOD awakened.
The Queen, she gives birth
To a new perfect human
That will bring you rebirth!

I have a message,
A message from GOD:
The womb of the Queen
Will bring you the vessel of blood.

The Queen, she has birthed him.
She has given him life.
The true human standing
To remove all your strife!

Mercury rising,
The message from GOD,
To show us the wings
Of the true man with the ROD!

THE PROPHECIES

❝

She gave birth to a son, a male child,
Who will rule all the nations with an iron scepter.
And her child was snatched up to
God and to his throne.

❞

- Revelation 12:5 (NIV)

❝

That one 'will rule them with an iron scepter
and will dash them to pieces like pottery' -
Just as I have received authority from my Father.

❞

- Revelation 2:27 (NIV)

RISING FROM THE ASHES

8 OF CUPS REVERSED

Rise, o' dear feminine!
Rise in your wake.
Rise from bad forces
And the ones who are fake.

Rise, o' dear feminine!
Rise from your sleep.
They have woken your giant,
But you no longer weep.

Rise, o' dear feminine!
Remove all your sin.
For your people are calling.
Shine your light from within.

Rise, o' dear feminine!
Rise in your glory.
For the people need you
To tell them your story.

Rise, o' dear feminine!
Find your strength now.
For GOD, He is calling
For you to give vow.

Vow to your people.
Vow for your truth.
Vow for your testimony.
Vow for your youth.

Rise, o' dear feminine!
They can no longer harm.
For you have the strength
Of GOD in your arm.

SUN SELF: SHOW YOUR TRUE SELF

THE MOON

Show me your scars,
And I will show you the way.
I will turn darkness
Into a new day.

Show me your true self.
Show me your face.
Show me your suffering
And show me your place.

Show me your sun,
And I'll show you my moon.
Show me your shadows,
And to you I will swoon **(kneel in awe).**

Find your true self **(in me).**
Find your true light.
Find yourself shining
In my **(twin flame)** mirror so bright.

I am a dark angel
That was burned from the men
Who created my shadows,
But I rise now again!

I am the real self,
The shadow of truth.
I am her, Magdalene,
Created in youth **(this life)**.

I am the woman
Who will serve GOD best.
For I am the true self
That has passed every test.

I am the fire,
The wind and the earth.
I am the mother
Of your soul in rebirth.

I am the sun,
The stars and the moon.
For I am now waking
From my hidden cocoon.

I am the shadow self,
But now I am three.
United with GOD
In true unity!

THE FUTURE IS HERE: TRUE UNITY

THE WORLD REVERSED

The world, it is turning,
For many still sleep.
The women of torture,
How I hear them all weep.

Awaken, O' feminine!
Awaken, divine,
To bring a new age
Of enlightening time.

The true world, I see it,
But the vision is bleak.
For many around me,
O' how they are weak.

GOD, hear my calling.
I wish to reverse
The evil around us
And the scorn woman's curse.

Arise now, great feminine!
Arise now, divine,
To bring new enlightenment
In space and in time.

My son, he is coming soon.
I feel him in womb.
To bring forth a new day
And create a new moon.

My son, he is coming now
To present the true rod,
To create a new world
And create a new blood.

The pure man, he will be.
The pure essence of life.
For he will give honour
To all women in strife.

The world, it is ending near,
But our new world will create
A true destined virtual plane
Of midheaven in fate!

THE FUTURE IS HERE: YOUR CALLING

THE HIGH PRIESTESS

A woman of truth.
A woman of life.
A woman from sufferance.
A woman from strife.

A woman with essence
Of truth and of GOD.
A woman who will carry
The Heir with his ROD.

A woman of vision.
A woman of fate.
A woman of unity
To bring a new date.

A woman with virtue.
A woman cut from the rest.
A woman who knows
Of no limit or test.

She will bring you truth.
She will bring you light.
She will bring you the book
That will lead in your fight.

A woman so pure.

A woman with GOD.

She will give you your saviour

Who will rule with a ROD.

PSALM 9

REMOVING YOUR CURSE
REVEALING YOUR LIGHT

19th of May, 2019

DAY AFTER FULL MOON PURGE

THE TOWER REVERSED

Today is the day
That you will learn
The many faces of woman
And the gift in the burn **(awakening).**

You have learned how to grow.
You have found your new peace
From burning your sins
And moving with ease.

The many awake
Are the ones who are saved,
But in your awakening
You must seek to be brave.

For when you awaken,
This is the true test.
To be removed from your sins
And become your true best!

The removal of sins
Is your blessing from curse,
From striving to be
Your true best from worst.

My dear, you are saved!
Rejoice in this day.
For this is your new life
In this new day of MAY.

You have found your true light.
You have battled with scars.
But now you are able
To unite Venus with Mars
(divine masculine and feminine energies).

My dear, you are blessed!
You have removed the great curse.
For your knowledge awakened you
In your seeking and thirst.

Do you not see your power
Was always hidden inside?
It was just covered in sin,
In great ego and pride.

But now you are healed,
You are balanced, restored.
And today you will find
All that you wish for and more.

For the GODS, how they've blessed you.
For the GODS, they do wake.
For they see your great vow
And your true love keepsake.

I am but your angel
That you've sought in despair,
But now you are the angel
That will flow through the air.

My dear, hear your power.
My dear, see the light!
My dear, you have mission
To burn your star bright.

You are now healed within.
You are now your true best.
But now you must give
This truth to the rest.

You are now an angel.
You are without taint.
You have been anointed
From sinner to saint.

You have removed this false curse
And revealed your true light.
My dear, you have awakened
And redeemed your true sight!

THE MESSAGE FOR YOU: THE FOUNTAIN OF YOUTH

PAGE OF SWORDS REVERSED

I have a message,
A message for you:
This is your true calling.
The fountain of youth!

You are the bearer of children
That will be born blessed.
For you have become saint
And passed every test.

I have a message,
A message for you:
That you will bear witness
To the bible of truth.

You are the true messenger
Of GOD and of light.
In this, you will show
Your true vision and sight.

I have a message,
And it is from GOD:
That you are the redeemer
Who will defy all the odds.

In this, you will show
Your battles, your scars.
You will show your merged energies
From Venus to Mars.

You will unite forces.
You will be the light.
For you will stand tall
As a star who shines bright.

Fight the false darkness
Of the ages and now,
For you will bring forth
A true vision in VOW.

A vow to the GODS
Who are with you in soul,
Who are blessing your mission
To bring others to whole.

I have a message,
And this is real, this is true:
You will be the giver of
The fountain of YOUTH.

DESTINY AND FATE

WHEEL OF FORTUNE REVERSED

The wheel, it is spinning.
The wheel, it is fate.
The wheel is your guidance
For you to create.

The wheel, it is spinning.
Can you not feel the air?
The wheel, it is changing
Your life from despair.

The wheel, it is showing
The light and the way.
To move to your north star
And present a new day.

The wheel, it is showing
Your destiny, fate.
The wheel, it is calling
For you to CREATE.

Find your true mission
Is revealed in the text.
The wheel is your guidance.
For the wheel, it is blessed.

The wheel tells your story
And reveals your true goal:
To bring forth your destiny
And bring you to whole.

The energies showing
In the wheel as it spins.
But what you must see
Is the true light within!

Do not be diluted
by the energies now.
For they will all merge
In your true essence in VOW.

The wheel is your guidance.
This is your true tool
To guide in your mission
And not be the fool.

Use this true element
That others reject
So you can merge energies
And be a true intellect!

The wheel, it is turning.
It's turning for you.
For you are with destiny.
You now know your TRUTH!

MESSENGER OF GOD

KNIGHT OF CUPS

You are the message,
The message from GOD.
You have defied gravity
And beat all the odds.

You are the true messenger.
You must be revealed!
For you are now whole,
And you have been healed.

You must keep your shield
And your cup in true tact.
For there is still great evil,
And this is a fact.

But you must be brave.
You must be the truth.
For you have a cup
And a fountain of YOUTH!

You have to show this
To the rest of the world.
For your story, it needs
To be shown and be heard.

There are many suffering
In your shoes and your path.
You must show true empathy

So you can give them an ARC
(a safe haven, like Noah's arc).

In your message from GOD,
You will truly reveal
You are cured of sin.
In this, you are sealed.

You are the true light,
The night and the day.
You will bring many
To their path and their way.

You will redeem others
As I have redeemed you,
And you will bring forth
A fountain of YOUTH!

A new age, it is coming.
Do you not see the light?
You are one of the angels
That must be in true sight.

Reveal yourself now
And reveal your true gifts!
For this is a grey battle
(Kriselda means grey battle)
And many still drift.

You must find your strength
And your will in your CALL!
You must be confident.
You must truly stand tall!

You are the message,
The fountain of youth.
You are the creator of
The sun in your truth.

This cup you must give
To others in wait
(waiting to be saved).
For this is your calling
And your message in fate.

You will find others
To help you in fight,
To create a new day
And bring forth true sight.

You are the message,
The message from GOD.
You must hold your head high
And bring forth the ROD!

PSALM 10

AWAKENED IN TRUTH
ELEMENTS UNITED

19ᵗʰ of May, 2019

UNITED IN FOUR CORNERS: CARRYING YOUR CROSS

4 OF WANDS x PAGE OF PENTACLES

United in vision.
United in sight.
United with eye.
United in fight.

You have united your corners,
You have united the air,
You have become one,
And removed the false glare.

Awakened in truth!
Awakened in light!
Awakened in unity!
And now, you've great sight.

My dear, here's your present,
Your gift from the GODS.
For you have defied
And beat all the ODDS.

You are the true miracle
That others will see.
And in this true miracle,
You have been set free.

You are but an angel
That burned through despair **(ashes).**
But today, you have woken
And removed the false glare.

My dear, you are 'wakened!
You have become light!
You have become saint
With no sinner in sight!

This is your great gift
And removal from curse.
For you have been anointed
With the four corners of earth.

My dear, you stand tall.
You are now living your dream.
For you are an angel
And your sins have wiped clean.

My dear, here's your gift.
This is your true light.
For you sought the truth
And awakened in sight!

TWO BECOME ONE IN UNITY

2 OF CUPS REVERSED

You have transformed.
You have truly healed.
Your true essence
Has now been revealed.

You have become light.
You have become day.
You have carried your cross
And come from the grey **(matter)**.

Rejoice now in unity.
Rejoice in delight.
For this is a battle
You've won in true sight!

Your two divine energies,
O' how they've become one.
You've revealed your true moon
And have become SUN.

My dear, you are saved.
You are blessed. You are fair.
You have created
A new life from despair.

Arose from the ashes
And settled the dust.
You have turned to your virtues
From false sin and of lust.

Today, you are beautiful.
My dear, you have wings!
You must show you are miracle
As a Queen for the Kings.

United in energies,
You are now repaired.
But now you must go forth
And produce a new heir.

A perfect human OF being.
A perfect one who is whole.
United since birth
And created from soul.

My dear, you will go forth
And create a new life.
A true youth in purity,
For you are GOD's wife.

For you are the Queen,
The mother of heir.
For you are the one
Who is true, who is fair
(fairest one of them all).

TRUE ABUNDANCE

10 OF PENTACLES

Abundance is calling.
Abundance is clear.
Abundance is happening.
Can you not see, my dear?

Abundance, you've created.
Abundance from light.
Abundance from being
The truth in plain sight!

Abundance, you see it.
Abundance, it's there.
Abundance for all,
For the Queen is so fair.

Abundance in love.
Abundance in health.
Abundance in family.
Abundance in wealth.

Abundance in gifts.
Abundance in skill.
Abundance in lifestyle.
Abundance in thrill.

Abundance awakened!
Abundance redeemed.
For you are the gold one,
Abundance of Queens!

VIRTUES IN VOW

THE HANGED MAN

Today is your day
Of true virtue in vow.
You have sought GOD,
And here she is now!
(The Dao, the way)

You've prayed every day,
And you've remained chaste.
All of your suffering
Did not go to waste.

You've now become alchemy,
For now you are one.
Virtues in vow,
You've created your SUN!

Do you not see the treasure
That you sought was within?
Through burning your sufferance
And revealing your sins?

In this, you have found
The true virtues from vice.
You have become saint
And turned naughty to nice.

This is your true calling:
To bring forth your soul
To others who need
Redeeming in whole.

This is your true virtue,
This is your true vow:
To create saints from sinners
And give them their crown.

My dear, they are waiting.
They are waiting for you
To bring a new day
And awaken in truth!

BLESSING THE CURSE: MIRACLE IN REBIRTH

QUEEN OF PENTACLES REVERSED

My dear, you have vision!
My dear, you have sight!
In this, you have won
The true battle in fight.

My dear, the great evil
Was covered in curse.
You were in true suffering,
Becoming your worst **(enemy).**

But now, you've come out
From the smoke and the dust,
Creating new day
From the ashes of lust **(greed, vice, sin).**

My dear, you are **PHOENIX.**
You rose from it all!
And in this true battle,
You've won. You stand tall!

Here are your blessings
That came from your curse.
Redeemed from true sufferance,
You lived through the worst.

You crossed your own **JORDAN (river),**
But you've now redeemed sight!
For your **ANJA (ajna)** awakened you
And gave you true LIGHT!

This is your true blessing
That came from your curse.
Your children in arms
Gave you true rebirth!

You are now a Queen!
You are now true light.
For you have recovered
From the battle and fight!

Your soul is redeemed.
You now live your truth.
You are the giver
Of the fountain of youth.

Your children, they've blessed you.
Do you not see you've won?
For you have in your womb
The truth, your son **(sun).**

In this sun **(son),** you are blessed!
This is your gift from your curse:
To create a new day
And a new universe.

Do you not see it coming
From within you, in light?
For this is your miracle,
A pure son **(sun)** from your fight!

You now know the truth,
The light and the way.
Now you can move forth
And create a new DAY!

PSALM 11

HEAR YE THE KING!

20th of May, 2019

THE CHOSEN ONE

KING OF PENTACLES

Hark! The herald
Angels sing!
Today is the day
There is a new king!

Hark! The herald
Angels sing!
Today is the day
When you unite in two wings!

Hark! The herald
Angels soar!
Today is the day
United from four.

Hark! The herald
Animals herd.
There is a new king.
Open the door!

Here is the mighty!
Here is the blessed!
Here are the ones who have
Passed every test!

Here is the king.
He now lights the way!
Here are your blessings,
Turned night into day!

Today you will see
Two souls, they unite!
For they have both passed
The judgement and fight!

Today is the day
That the kingdom will soar.
For the King and the Queen,
They unite whole from four.

See the true light.
See the divine.
See the new life
In a cup of new wine!

The new blood is here.
It is here now to stay.
For the darkness is faded,
Turned night into day!

Today is the day
That you will see
A kingdom awakened
And many are free!

Hark! The herald.
Hear the King!
Who holds the true sceptre,
The crown and the ring!

PERFECT KINGDOM:
RESTORATION OF EDEN!

PAGE OF SWORDS REVERSED
x 10 OF CUPS

Listen to this:
Can you hear the bird?
It is singing a melody
For all to be heard!

Listen to this:
Can you hear the sweet song?
A melody of an angel,
So sharp and so long.

Listen to this:
Can you see the new light
That this King has brought
With his Queen, in true sight?

Listen to this:
There is a trumpet I hear!
A new Kingdom awaiting.
No long shall we fear!

Listen to this:
A perfect kingdom in sight.
We have won the true battle
And recovered from fight!

Listen to this:
I am the message from GOD.
Follow the man
With the sceptre and ROD!

He will bring you to light.
He will bring you to day.
He will show you the kingdom
And show you the way!

Listen to this,
And listen right now:
You are in judgement.
You must keep your vow
(of chastity, virtues).

Hear the great trumpets.
Hear the great song.
For the road, it is promised,
Even though it is long!

Find your true destiny
And fate, It awaits
In entering EDEN,
Restored through the gates!

SEEK YE THE TREASURE!

4 OF PENTACLES REVERSED

Seek ye the treasure.
In the gates, it awaits.
For the jewels, they are promised
In true vision and faith.

Seek ye the treasure.
It will restore your dark soul,
And bring you to oneness,
And again, become whole!

Seek ye the treasure.
The judgement is here.
Will you find it through love
Or falter through fear?

Seek ye the treasure.
The crystal is clear,
To bring you new beginnings
In abundance, my dear!

Seek ye the treasure.
The kingdom awaits.
King and Queen are providing
For the believers of fate!

Seek ye the treasure—
The gold, silver, glass,
The crystals, the jewels,
The fountain, the brass.

Seek ye the treasure.
In your soul, it awaits,
But first you must pass
The battle of only the great
(battle of good and evil).

THE KING OF KINGS

REVELATION 19:16
KING OF CUPS

"

On his robe and on his thigh he has this name written:
King of kings and lord of lords.

"

- Revelation 19:16 (NIV)

King of cups.
King of life.
King of virtue.
Redeemer of strife.

King of Kings.
King of heir.
King of fire.
King of air.

King of promise.
King of land.
King with the rod.
King so grand.

King of kingdom.
King of thrones.
King of the wealthy.
King of homes.

King, the redeemer.
King, hear my call.
Deliver us now
From the wake of the fall.

King, give us virtue.
To you, we do stand.
King, give us freedom.
Our life in your hands.

King, you are honoured.
King, you are blessed.
King, you are true light,
A cut from the rest.

King, you are true.
King, you are whole.
King, we believe you
To unite with our soul!

THE QUEEN OF QUEENS

QUEEN OF CUPS

Queen of honour.
Queen so fair.
Queen of water.
Queen of air.

Queen of life.
Queen of truth.
Queen of rebirth.
Queen of youth.

Queen of Queens.
Queen to heir.
Queen of virtue.
Queen so rare.

Queen so beautiful.
Queen so bright.
Queen of the sun **(son)**.
Queen so bright!

Queen, you are loved.
Queen, you are whole.
Queen, you deliver
Us from our dark soul!

Queen of abundance.
Queen, you are true.
Queen, you bring brightness
And make our skies blue.

Queen, you are magic.
Queen, you are light.
Queen, you are glistening,
A star shining bright!

Queen of the crystals.
Queen of the gold.
Queen of immortals.
Queen of the bold!

Queen of the Queens.
Queen of the knights.
Queen of the Kings.
Queen of great sight!

THE LOVERS RESTORED IN THE GARDEN OF EDEN

THE LOVERS REVERSED

Enter the gates,
For heaven awaits!
My dear, you are blessed.
You have passed every test!

Your equal awaits you.
The lovers, restored
From a lifetime of suffering,
Lost battles, and swords.

Today is the day
When your true love awaits.
The kingdom is calling you
And opened the gates!

Overflowing with riches,
Abundance is clear.
For you've conquered great darkness
And conquered your fears!

My brave one, you're welcome
In this place to call home!
In uniting your love
And reclaiming your throne!

I am just a vessel.
So in me, hear GOD.
You must keep your great virtues
And hold up your ROD!

Victory, it is conquered.
My dear, you are truth —
Presenting new day
With the fountain of youth!

No long will you suffer.
No long will you fear.
For you only see love
And the light from your tears.

Redemption is yours,
Redemption in fate.
Now enter your kingdom.
Your truth, it awaits!

A POWER OF THRONE

THE FOOL REVERSED

The fool in reverse
Is the one who is blessed.
For in new beginnings,
He's passed every test.

The fool in reverse
Is the one who has broke
Every curse and great suffering
In himself. He has woke.

A great giant of virtue
Restored his lost soul.
He has redeemed failures
And now become whole.

The fool in reverse
Is a great man, indeed.
He has unpacked his burdens
And taken GOD's heed.

The fool in reverse
Is the one will bring
A new sound and a melody
Of new life when he sings.

The fool in reverse;
He was lost, now he's found—
Recovered his battles
And found a new ground.

On top of the mountains,
O' lord, hear him roar!
On top of the clouds,
O' wow, see him soar!

He has become angel
And a true vision in sight,
Become a true star
Burning and shining so bright!

Listen, he's singing,
The fool in reverse.
You can hear the great angels
In every song, every verse.

He sits on his throne,
He wears a long gown
Covered in crystals,
And wears now, the crown!

Power to the fool
That you laughed in true spite.
For now, this fool owns
Every treasure in sight.

The true man he is.
O' this fool, how he's pure.
For he overcame obstacles
And found his own cure.

A power of wisdom.
A power of sight.
A power of voice.
A power of might.

A power in victory.
A power to own.
A power in destiny.
A power of THRONE.

PSALM 12

HEALER OF THE LIGHT

21st of May, 2019

THE STAR

THE STAR

Healer of the light.
Healer of the day.
Healer from the night.
Healer, show the way!

Healer, you are blessed.
Healer, you do soar.
Healer, please show us
The guidance through the door.

Healer, where's the key?
Healer, show the light.
Healer, please show me
The armour to stand fight!

Healer, I am weak,
But healer, you are strong.
Healer, keep me focused
On the path, for it is long.

Healer, show the way.
Healer, I need you.
Healer, I need guidance
To the door to walk on through.

Healer, I feel warm.
In your love, I do feel healed.
Healer, you are the one,
The light and truth revealed!

BALANCE, VICTORY AND PEACE

JUSTICE

Today is the day
In which I have learned
There are many sins
In the man to be burned.

Today is the day
In which I bow down,
For I have found GOD in you,
The one who wears the crown.

Today is the day
In which I feel blessed.
For I feel the truth
In my heart, in my chest.

Today is the day
In which I am healed
From suffering, vice,
From sin and of greed.

Today is the day
In which I am sworn
To now become whole
From being so torn.

Today is the day
In which fate is sealed,
For my true light is shining,
My true self revealed!

TWIN SOULS UNITE

2 OF CUPS

We have come together.
We have won the fight!
Twin souls awakened,
United through light.

We have come together.
We now both stand tall.
We have recovered from battle,
Risen from the great fall.

We have come together.
Our true youth revealed.
For our twin souls awakened,
Recovered and healed.

We have come together
In mind and in chest.
For our twin souls united,
And now we are blessed!

We have come together
In mind and in soul.
United in energies,
And now become whole.

We have come together.
Our true self revealed.
For our two minds united.
Now our fate is sealed!

THE HANGED MAN, REVEALED!

THE HANGED MAN

The hanged man, I see you.
The hanged man, revealed.
The hanged man, I know you.
The hanged man is healed.

The hanged man, he 'wakens.
The hanged man on tree.
The hanged man, shine your light
In knowledge from me.

I see you have suffered.
Your dark knight revealed.
But your crown, it awakens
Because you are healed!

The hanged man, come down now.
Remove all your ties.
You can see now, so clearly,
Through the mist of the lies!

The hanged man, you're shining!
I see your true light.
For you have removed yourself
From the burdens of fight.

The hanged man, I heal you.
The hanged man is blessed.
For he has found sufferance,
Yet passed every test.

The hanged man, come down now!
There's no need to hide.
For you have reduced yourself
From sin and from pride.

The hanged man, I see you!
Your shine is so bright.
For you have redeemed yourself
In the healing of light!

THE SHIELD FROM THE CURSE: PURE LIGHT

KNIGHT OF WAND REVERSED

Knight of wand
In reverse,
You are my shield
From every curse.

You have found truth,
Resolved inner fight.
Please protect me
In day and night.

Knight of wand,
I take your heed.
You have been blessed,
And thus, decreed **(anointed by GOD).**

Knight of wand,
You do protect.
For you have found
True intellect.

Knight of wand,
Protect my soul.
Use your shield
To keep me whole.

Knight of wand,
O' how you're blessed!
For you've found life
Inside your chest.

Knight of wand,
You are my knight.
In shining armour,
Turn day from night.

Knight of wand,
You do stand ground.
For you hold the wand
And have heard the sound.

The trumpets calling
For you to protect
The many like me
Who've suffered and wept.

Knight of wand,
Remove the curse.
Please shield my heart
To keep me on course.

Knight of wand,
Please show me the way.
For you are strong
And protect our day!

FALLEN ANGEL:
REDEEMER OF LIGHT!

JUDGEMENT REVERSED

Fallen angel.
Redeemer of light.
Slayer of dragons.
The wife of the night.

Fallen angel.
Soul now revealed.
Heart now whole.
Mind now healed!

Fallen angel,
You are blessed.
You are the one
To pass every test.

Fallen angel,
You are decreed.
You are with GOD,
And you are with seed.

Fallen angel,
The trumpets I hear.
Can you bring me to them
And remove me from fear?

Fallen angel,
You are so bright!
Your wings are so beautiful.
You are now pure light.

Fallen angel,
Judgement is here!
Can you play your sweet sound
And remove me from fear?

Fallen angel,
Awaken my soul!
I wish to be like you,
To become one and whole.

Fallen angel,
Your soul is so pure.
You've shined on us all
And given us cure.

Fallen angel, I hear you!
I am taking your heed
To remove all my suffering,
My guilt and my greed.

Fallen angel, please cure me
With your trumpets and sound.
Please rise me from sleeping
And create a new ground!

BLESS'D SOUL: WOUNDED HEALER OF THE LIGHT

4 OF CUPS

Bless'd are the meek.
Bless'd are the torn.
Bless'd is the woman
Who is marked with 6 in scorn.

Bless'd are the meek
From her sickness and her ail **(ment)**.
Bless'd is her sufferance.
For in GOD, she will not fail!

Bless'd is the woman
Who is seeking to be whole.
For in this, you will find me
As the healer of your soul!

Bless'd is your battle.
Bless'd is your mark **(666)**.
For the dragon you are slaying
To reveal the truth and arc **(arcanum)**.

Bless'd is your mission.
Bless'd is your fight.
For now you've been anointed,
Wounded healer of the light!

THE SCARLET WOMAN SLAY'D THE BEAST

REVELATION 13
THE DEVIL REVERSED

Scarlet woman, you are marked
And your number is revealed! **(666),**
But you must own your number
In order to be healed!

The beast is strong in number,
And he is hidden from plain sight.
But Scarlet, you are stronger!
You must stand and win this fight!

The GODS, they do protect you
And watch your every move.
Do not fall in relapse
Or your soul will be removed!

Scarlet woman, you are tainted;
And your soul, it lies in sleep.
You must look aside from suffering.
For your soul is there. Dig deep!

Scarlet woman, I see demons
Inside you every day.
You must fight to win this battle
And remove your sins in slay!

Scarlet woman, see your virtues.
They are deep within your soul.
For even the worst sinners
Are able to be whole!

Scarlet woman, see your wisdom
From your suffering and scorn.
Because GOD can heal your demons
That have made you become torn!

Scarlet woman, find the freedom
That lives within your CHRIST **(seed consciousness).**
For in this union, you will find
Your soul reborn in THRICE **(trinity, union).**

Christ is Reborn in Unity.

PSALM 13

REJOICE, REJOICE!

22nd of May, 2019

ABUNDANCE IN GIVING

ACE OF PENTACLES

Today is a day
For the meek who are living.
Today is a day
That is a day full of giving!

Today is a day
When our hearts are now pure.
Today is a day
When our life is now cured.

Rejoice, o' great healer!
For in your name, we bow down.
For giving us life again
And reviving the crown!

Rejoice, o' great mother!
For your lineage is blessed.
You have given us life again
And created the best!

Rejoice in abundance now.
We are full of life!
Removed all our fears and sins
And removed us from strife!

Rejoice, o' my love, my DAO.
For in your name, we do live.
We have so much to offer now
And so much to give!

Our hearts are so full and pure.
Our lives are so right.
You have saved us from suffering
And brought us to light!

Abundance is here and now.
We see the great gold.
For you have opened the gates,
Giving us coin to hold!

THE LOVERS UNITED!

THE LOVERS

Rejoice, rejoice!!
I see now the light!
Rejoice, rejoice!!
We have won the great fight!

Rejoice, rejoice!!
Can you see? We are bound **(in unity).**
Rejoice, rejoice!!
We were lost, now we're found!

Rejoice, rejoice!!
We are merged now in one.
Rejoice, rejoice!!
We have found the new SUN.

Rejoice, rejoice!!
The new world is now here!
Rejoice, rejoice!!
The Garden of Eden is clear.

Rejoice, rejoice!!
The true lovers unite.
Rejoice, rejoice!!
The phoenix rising new heights!

Rejoice, rejoice!!
Adam, now back with Eve.
Rejoice, rejoice!!
A new day now achieved.

Rejoice, rejoice!!
The second coming is now.
Rejoice, rejoice!!
We are taking new VOW **(in Christ).**

Rejoice, rejoice!!
We have found now the truth.
Rejoice, rejoice!!
Restored in the fountain of youth.

THE SUN GOD

THE FOOL REVERSED

Hello! Hello from GOD!
It's me again!
Hello! Hello from GOD!
I have a message to send.

Hello! Hello from GOD!
The SUN now is here.
Hello! Hello from GOD!
A new vision, it's clear.

The fool, he is walking.
So bright is the way.
For the fool, he is journeying
To a new world, a new day!

The fool, o' how he's tall and proud.
For the fool, he's with GOD.
Walking in the new day and sun,
He follows the ROD.

GOD, he is with right now.
He follows the SUN,
Restoring his energies
And merging to one!

The fool, he rejoices clear.
The fool, he is woke.
The fool, he is reborn as
The man with new cloak.

Hello! Hello from GOD!
The fool, he becomes son.
The son to the GOD of SUN
Now merged into one!

The fool is the messenger.
The message from GOD:
To follow the light and way,
And follow the ROD!

PSALM 14

REVEAL A NEW WORLD

22nd of May, 2019

JUDGEMENT IS HERE

JUDGEMENT

There is an evil
That exists in this world.
There is good and bad,
But the truth will be heard!

The trumpets are calling
The fear in reverse.
For GOD is the way
To lift you from curse.

Reveal a new world.
Reveal your true soul.
Reveal your true essence
In truth and in whole.

Remove now the veil
That exists from the curse.
For the energies you have
Create a new universe!

The light, it is here now.
The light, it is truth.
It reveals you from darkness.
It restores you in youth.

A lifetime of suffering
Is now formed in gold.
All of your heartache
Will create a new world.

Today is your reckoning
Of the death of your sins.
For the evil is burned from you,
And a new light shines within!

BLESSINGS OF THE SOUL

6 OF CUPS

Bless my journey.
Bless my light.
Bless my vision.
Bless my sight.

Bless my fortune.
Remove me from stare.
Bless me from curses.
Remove me from glare.

Bless my new energy.
Remove my old stains.
Bless my new happiness.
Bless my old pain.

Bless my old demons.
Reveal my true light.
Bless my old enemies.
Assist them in fight
(of their own demons).

Bless this new world.
Bless my new life.
Bless my new home.
Bless me from strife.

Bless my family.
Bless my true friends.
Bless, too, my enemies;
May they seek amends.

Bless my pure heart and soul.
Bless my new sun.
Bless my journey
In becoming the one.

Bless the new future
And fountain of youth.
Bless all our children,
Because they are the TRUTH!

RESTORE THE PURE SOUL

THE STAR

Restore now our vision
And our true love in sight.
Restore now our soul
And conquer the fight.

Restore now our livelihood.
Restore us in youth.
Restore us in love,
For this love is the TRUTH.

Restore us in essence.
Reveal our pure light.
Find now our heaven
Is now in plain sight.

Restore our true spirit.
Reveal now the way.
Show us the SUN.
Turn night into day.

Find now our enemies
And demons in fight.
Restore them, o' heavenly,
In their divine light.

The many around me,
O' how they're stained.
But in these true blessings,
May their light be remained.

Restore the pure soul, my GOD.
Help us gain strength.
Bless now our journey
In time and in length.

PSALM 15

SEEK YE THE FREEDOM!

22nd of May, 2019

KARMIC LESSONS

2 OF PENTACLES

The resolve in your karma,
It truly is great.
For in this resolve,
You will find your true fate.

You will be just pure love.
With demons, no more.
You will surely create
And open the door.

The heavens await.
Gates open and flood.
The new mind and body
Filled with new blood.

Christ seed awakening,
Resolved from the wake.
Redeeming our destiny,
Our future we make.

Our karma is now resolved.
Our soul is restored.
Our true self awaits us.
We have now cut the cord.

Summon our energies
To resolve karma through light.
This is a true battle.
We will win the fight!

Today is the reckoning **(fate, judgement)**
When we will attest
That through GOD and destiny,
We will pass every test.

Forever is clear right now.
In heaven, we see.
For karma has disappeared.
We've crossed the red sea **(Jordan River)**.

Our karmic loop is a hell
That has trapped our pure soul.
But when we listen close,
We will hear our GOD call.

Seek ye the freedom now!
Seek it from light.
For in karmic reckoning,
Our vision is bright!

PSALM 16

REBIRTH OF THE NEW WORLD

23rd of May, 2019

NORTH NODE STAR

STAR x 9 OF SWORDS REVERSED

There is a secret
That many don't know.
There exists other worlds
In which we can grow.

We live here on earth,
But there are the stars.
There are other planets
From Venus to Mars.

We must find our placement
On the map, as it shows
There are many paths
In which we can flow.

What we must seek
Is to find our true way.
Look at the north node
To turn dreams into day.

The sun, it is set
In our map and our node.
What we must strive
Is to find our true mode!

We have many gifts.
We have many dreams.
What we must now find
Is our true path and the stream.

We have many distractions
That lay in our way.
But the one who succeeds
Turns night into day **(moon into sun).**

We must bring our consciousness
To light and to truth.
For this will reveal
Our true calling and youth.

You are just a vessel,
A product of GOD,
A true product of rebirth
In the stars and new blood.

THE TRUE STAR CALLING

8 OF CUPS x 7 OF PENTACLES

You find now, your freedom.
In stars, it awaits.
The other realm calling
For you now, in fate!

This is your true destiny:
To be one with stars.
After searching so long,
Venus now is with Mars.

United in freedom.
United in soul.
United in rebirth.
Now finally whole.

You are now awakened
As a spirit and star.
You are able to travel
So wide and so far.

Your destiny calling.
Can you see it awaits?
You are now in your true node.
Your path, it is fate!

The seventh of angels
(Revelation 8:2 NIV),
You are in the blood
Of the ones who are chosen
To lead with a ROD.

You must know your calling:
To open the gates.
For you will bring forth
A new world, a new state.

Your path to true freedom.
The gates open wide.
For you are the chosen one
To bear a true child.

The twelve stars, they twinkle
On empress with GOD.
You will be the one
To bring the truth with the ROD
(Revelation 12 NIV).

LOSE YOUR WAY, FIND YOUR SOUL

ACE OF PENTACLES REVERSED

A woman of destiny,
You are one with your soul.
You had been so broken,
But now you are whole.

A woman of destiny,
To be one with divine.
You bring forth a new child
In space and in time.

A woman of destiny,
You have a true fate:
To bring a new day
And bring a new state.

Empire calling.
Victory is so clear.
State of abundance.
The new world, it is near.

Your calling as healer,
As the truth and as life.
You are GOD and rebirth,
The redeemer of strife.

Lost your way from the shadows.
But in this, now you are whole.
Woman of destiny,
You redeem all lost souls.

THE NEW WORLD AWAITS!

KNIGHT OF WANDS

Find your true calling.
Find your true fate.
Find your true destiny.
The new world awaits!

Knight of wands, he is leading.
This man is your son,
The one who will bring
A new world back to ONE.

He leads with your vision.
He is guided by you.
For you are his compass,
And you are his truth.

This man is your destiny,
For he is your heir.
He will set forth a new world,
And a new land and air.

Set forth now in calling,
For you are with child.
You must seek to protect him
From the beast and the wild
(Revelation 12:5 NIV).

The woman of calling,
You are clothed now in SUN.
To set forth in rebirth,
To present a new SON.

He is the true saviour,
Redeemer in fate.
For he is THE ONE
The new world awaits!

GENESIS: A NEW
WORLD IN REBIRTH

7 OF CUPS REVERSED

You are the mother,
Mother of earth.
And now you are with GOD
Through the fate of rebirth.

You have rejoined forces.
Divine, you are one.
Now you can bring forth
True midheaven and SUN.

The is the beginning
Of a new way and life.
For you are now one with GOD.
You have become WIFE.

Set forth in true calling,
You will produce heir
To bring forth new water,
New earth, and new air.

The fire is burning.
The elements clear
To bring forth a new world
That exists without fear.

The garden of Eden,
O' how I see it restore!
To bring together a new world—
Elements of the four.

You are the redeemer
Of heaven and earth.
For you are the true mother
Of life in rebirth!

(UP OF LIFE

KNIGHT OF CUPS

Here it is!
Cup of life.
Here it is!
The cup from WIFE **(of GOD)**.

Here it is!
A brand new globe.
It is through her,
The woman robed.

Gemini Rising
To produce a new SUN **(son)**,
To bring forth the energies
And mould them as one.

Gemini Rising,
She holds now a cup.
To bring us to midheaven,
The only way up!

Gemini Rising,
She is the true sign
Of GOD and of unity,
As one with divine.

Gemini Rising,
A new life with no fear.
For in her cup of life,
The water is clear **(pure)**.

DARK ANGEL (PHOENIX) AWAKENED

GEMINI / MERCURY RISING
TEMPERANCE

Walking in the valley
Of the shadow of death,
I can hear the devil calling
Fear and tears that I've wept.

You wanna know the funny thing
about being dead?
Your body's so cold and numb
From the torture, tears wept.

But what they don't know is
That I am a new breed
Of the wives that are fallen,
Reborn from the seed.

You think that you've killed us?
Well, I got some news.
I am the dark angel
Coming back to haunt you.

Arise now. Awaken
The dark angels of GOD
Coming out through the fire
And holding the ROD!

You think that you've won?
Well, I've got some news.
Phoenix is rising,
A dark angel with bruises.

Beat down and tormented,
You men think you've won?
Well now we're back, haunting you.
Our work here ain't done.

This is the real message
That we have from GOD.
Just know that we're coming
Back with a great flood
(Noah's flood, second coming).

My womb and my children,
I live now for them.
From the torment of abuse
And disrespect from the men.

Fire is calling.
Redeem all your sins
Or burn in the fire.
Ima reveal you, FALSE KINGS.

Phoenix angels arising,
Coming out from the dark,
Awakened through **KRISTA (female Christ),**
Redeemed through the ark
**(Noah's ark, great arcanum,
book of life).**

New World Order is coming.
Yea, I got the seed.
Awaken, my angels.
We are the new breed!

HAIL MARY (MAGDALENE): TUPAC COVER

THE HIGH PRIESTESS

Come with me.
Hail MARY, please redeem...

I aint a devil,
But don't push me.
Revenge is like the sweetest joy.
Never giving p*ssy!

Picture paragraphs unloaded.
Wise words being coded.
Men are weakness in this rap game.
I sow it.

Bowed down, prayed to GOD,
Hoping he was listening.
All the cries, pain and torture.
Now I rise. Now I'm glistening.

Now pay attention.
Rest in peace mama, I'm a phoenix
In these killing fields.
Mama Mary, catch me if I go.

Let's go deep inside
My solitary mind of a mad woman.
All the demons in the dark **(how they hide).**
Evil lurks. Enemies see me bleed.

Activated my old hate.
Let it break to the flame.
Set trip, empty out my drip.
Never stop to aim.

Some say the game
Is all corrupted.
Well, I'm here slaying, still alive
After I had erupted.

Was finding solace in a drink
With no composure.
Never finding what I need
To give me closure.

Break; Hail Mary.

I was raising hell, 'cos the devil
Willed me in all his glory.
Put down, raped, shot down.
Now I'm back to tell a story.

Bowed down
To the devil incarnate.
You mutha f*kas pushed me
To a place when it wasn't fated
(not my destiny).

Now triple six **(666)** is my fate.
I embrace it.
Never one to avoid
Fear and sin incarnate.

There's no end to this shame.
Voices of the fallen, do you hear them?
Put to fend for themselves.
A victim to the system.

Single mother, sixteen.
This was real life.
You have no idea what it means
To be a dark wife.

How can I heal wounds
When I've been wounded?
Chiron fated, it was sealed
When I was founded.

You have no idea what it's like
To live this story.
All you men wanna know is
Your next quick hit, your own glory
(pride, ego).

Phoenix on the rise,
Back to tell a story.
Now it's fated, rising
To take back all the glory.

Listen to this prayer
I'm here saying.
Redeem me, Mama Mary.
Please, I'm praying...

PSALM 17

VICTORY EXALTED IN UNITY
THE CHOSEN ONES

24th of May, 2019
11.11AM

QUEEN OF KINGS

KING OF SWORDS

Yea, though I walk in the valley
Of the shadow of death
(Psalm 23:4 NIV),
I come back with true victory,
Leading the fallen who wept.

My sword, it is sharpened.
My sight is redeemed.
I have slay'd the great dragon
And become the true Queen!

Awakened from torture.
Awakened through light.
I moved through the battle
And won the great fight.

Forgive me, my highness **(false king)**,
For this now is my throne.
Queen rising to take back
What's mine. This, I own.

You tried to expel me,
But my lord, just you wait.
For you will be murdered
In cold blood. This is fate.

I'm the Queen. Hear me roaring.
I stand up and fight,
Recovered from demons,
Coming out from the night.

You cannot remove us,
The wives of nightfall.
For now we've united.
In one, we stand tall.

I lead now the army.
This is our true light.
To stand up to false kings.
To stand up and fight.

This is our true victory.
We've won in true blood.
For we hold the virtues
Of female Christ and of GOD!

I am the high priestess
That you all tried to burn.
But now, I have risen
To put you false kings in urn.

HONOURING THE TRUE WOMAN

QUEEN OF WANDS x KING OF CUPS

A true Queen is honoured
With her true king by side.
He reduces his ego,
Reduces his pride.

A true king is humble.
He allows her to rule.
For he knows she does hold
The rod, fire and fuel.

A true Queen awakened,
Revealing true sight.
For she has great vision,
Creating a new day from night.

A true king is patient.
He has passed every test.
Exalted from false kings,
He is cut from the rest.

A true Queen is admired.
She's restored the great land.
And with her, she holds
The great arc in her hand
(great arcanum, book of life).

Restored in true unity,
The twin souls unite
To stand up and win
This great battle and fight.

HIDDEN IN SACRED UNITY

2 OF CUPS REVERSED

The sacred unity
Of King and of Queen;
It is blessed through GOD
And everything and between.

The true love awakens
With true end in sight —
To win the great battle,
United to fight.

Together, they partner,
Equal in strength.
For the Queen has awakened
Her power in length.

No long is there suffering.
The people do love.
The King and Queen joined in unity
To become the true ONE.

Their hearts are awakened.
Their soul is restored.
Their energies moulded
To be one with the Source.

PAST LIVES IN KARMA: NEFERTITI'S LOST LOVE

2 OF PENTACLES REVERSED

I saw him in my dreams.
I saw him in fight.
He was my great love.
He was my true knight.

I loved him with essence.
I loved him in whole.
But I was the Queen.
He was my servant I wanted to hold.

Pharaoh so evil,
He ruined my land.
But with my true knight,
He did hold my hand.

We moved through the battles,
United in fight.
A sacred unity hidden
From the rest in plain sight.

I wish we could marry.
My heart, it was torn.
Pharaoh did kill him.
I wept with such scorn.

Redeem me, O' SUN GOD.
Please unite us this time.
I have cried in past lifetimes
For this true love of mine.

I see him this lifetime.
I know his true light.
Please help me to find him
So we can unite.

Karma is calling.
I pray every night
To find the true one
With wisdom and sight.

I know he is somewhere,
My twin flame in new youth **(this life)**.
SUN GOD, unite us.
For triple six **(666)** is our truth.

I know we sinned greatly,
But now we're redeemed.
Please recover our souls
To unite — **ELOHIM.**

THE ETERNAL OPTIMIST:
A FOOL IN LOVE

THE FOOL

True love awakened.
My heart does not rest.
I keep trying to find the one.
I'm a fool, but I'm bless'd.

My heart, it is aching.
I have heard his true song.
But my journey is still
So far and so long.

I see the rays, SUN GOD.
Please give me your light
To find my true love
And bring him to sight.

I'm an educated fool
Still hoping for love.
Recovered from misery,
But I see the true dove.

A new day awakened
My heart and my soul.
Find me the one
Who will bring me back whole.

The fool, I am branded.
For I know I have failed.
But eternal as optimist,
I know LOVE will prevail.

Please help me to find him.
My journey is bright.
I have recovered from demons.
Now seeking my knight.

Shining armour, I see him.
He is shielded by GOD.
Together, we can rule
Iron fist with a ROD.

In LOVE, all things possible.
I know this is true.
For GOD hath redeemed me
From being torn in two.

I am now seeking
The one whose journey is same.
For we will redeem our sins
In fortune and fame.

I know he is out there.
I know he is blessed.
I know he is anointed,
For he's passed every test.

Dear GOD, please bless me
On my journey to find.
For a fool, I am truly,
For this lost love of mine.

Twin flames united.

UNITED IN MISSION

8 OF PENTACLES

United in mission.
United in love.
United in purpose.
United as doves.

My heart is now pure.
But my heart, it does seek
The one who is humble,
The one who is meek.

We have the same virtues,
The same essence in GOD.
We are both redeemed.
Iron fist with a ROD.

My heart, it is calling
For this man to reveal
Himself to me in song.
In this, we will seal.

We share the same love.
We share the same light.
We share the same destiny.
We share the same fight.

Work hard in my gifts
And my virtues. I'm bless'd.
Removed all my curses
And pass every test.

I know in this, GOD
Will give me my great reward.
For the man who will come
Is the real one from the herd.

He is of true virtue,
Of GOD and of faith.
Both scorned with the 6,
But redeemed through the 8th **(infinity).**

PSALM 18

A LOVE OF A LIFETIME

24th of May, 2019

MY CHILDREN MY TRUTH

6 OF CUPS

Finding my truth.
Finding my peace.
Finding my life.
Move now with ease.

A love of a lifetime.
The love of my womb.
Love of my children.
This is my real truth.

O' how you bless me!
O' how I cry.
O' GOD, you saved me.
O' now I fly!

My wings are united
And mended as one.
My heart, it is wholesome.
My soul, now my SUN!

A love of a lifetime.
This is my true song.
Looking for love
When it was there all along.

O' GOD, how you're merciful.
I live now my dreams.
Finding my happiness.
My sunshine, it beams.

Light from my soul,
It comes now in rays.
Shining my truth,
Revealing new days.

This is my true destiny,
My womb and my youth.
My INDIGO children
Existing in truth.

My heart is so full.
O' GOD, how I cry.
My womb is so precious.
Now I can fly!

STARSEEDS

THE STAR

O' how you saved me.
O' how I cry.
My heart, how it flutters
Like a true butterfly.

My song, my true melody,
My true loves in life—
Redeem me from suffering,
Recovered from strife.

My heart, it awakens
To now become pure,
To lead me into heaven.
O' how demure.

The stars, they are shining.
O' how they do wait.
Looking for us
To join them in fate.

My children, my destiny,
My heart and my soul—
You have saved my existence
And brought me to whole.

A love of a lifetime.
A love through the age.
Find us twinkling
On the centre stage.

Seeing my heart in them.
Seeing them dream.
Seeing them soar.
Seeing them beam.

Rays of sunshine.
Rays of light.
Rays of purity
Turn day from night.

My children of purity,
You will soar in true heights.
My wings from adversity,
You gave me true sight.

The clouds, they are waiting
For us to create.
Earth merged with heaven,
We all ELEV8!

PSALM 19

THE GREAT STRENGTH WITHIN DILIGENCE IN VIRTUE

25th of May, 2019

GIFTS FROM GOD

STRENGTH

There is a great gift
That I am giving to you:
The gift of awakening
In wisdom and truth.

You are a true angel
Awakened from GOD.
You have a true mission
To lead with the ROD.

If you wish for security,
You must listen true.
This is my mission
I'm entrusting to you.

You are marked with the beast
Of triple six **(Revelation 13:18 NIV).**
But in defeating this beast,
You will seal your true gifts.

You will receive music.
You will receive song.
You will receive abundance
As if it was there all along.

You are a true healer.
A message from GOD:
You will be a true leader,
A writer of LOVE!

Please know you must listen,
For you are of fate.
Don't doubt your true gifts,
Or your true essence and state!

Reveal your true being.
Reveal yourself true.
You must listen to me
In this mission for you.

You are a true messenger,
You are of true love,
You are a true healer,
And you are a true dove!

Your children, they are your gold.
Remember this now.
For in this, you must keep
Your spirit in vow.

Do not follow money.
Do not follow fame.
Do not follow security
Or revive your old flames.

Today is your truest self.
Your essence is pure.
Your new world is awaiting.
No fall to endure.

You must be strong within
To heal yourself now.
For in this, you will find your gifts
By holding your vow **(of chastity, purity).**

Do not look for others to do
What you can do yourself.
For you will be recovered
In health and in wealth.

Be grateful for all your gifts
And all of your woes.
For in this, you will reveal
Your true light and true glow.

You are a true angel
That was sent from above,
Sent to heal others
As the spirit and dove.

Your womb, it is strong and pure.
For the beast, it is tamed.
Now you are glistening;
And in this, you'll be famed.

Your trueness is legacy,
For your gifts shall reveal.
O' how they will be seen.
O' how they will heal!

Do not worry for money,
For the world will know you;
Know you are destined
And chosen from few.

Be honoured with strength within,
For you will stand tall.
Your abundance reveals itself
From your sufferance and fall.

Be diligent in your strength and gifts.
For this is your test:
To work hard each day and night.
To rise up to your best **(self)**!

DESTINY AWAITS YOU

IN VIRTUE AND TRUTH

Destiny awaits you,
Destiny in the stars.
You will unite energies
From Sun, Venus to Mars!

Your Chiron **(key)** is waiting
For you to behold.
The key to reveal your heart
Is yours to unfold!

You must use your healing
To unlock your gifts.
For my dear, there are many.
In this, do not drift!

Remain chaste in virtue.
Remain humbly confined.
Remain true and hidden.
Nurture your gifts of the mind.

In this, you must practice
And toil every day,
For there is still a beast in you.
But in work, you will slay!

Keep moving forward.
Perfect all your skills.
For the one who wins victory,
Is the one with true will.

Destiny waits
For you to be whole,
Reveal your true gifts,
And reveal your true soul!

This is GOD speaking.
I am here. Live your truth!
Bring forth your destiny.
In your heart, it awaits you!

PSALM 20

CONVERSATIONS WITH GOD
A MOTHER'S TRUE LOVE

25th of May, 2019

UNCONDITIONAL LOVE

A MOTHER'S LOVE
8 OF CUPS

Hello, my daughter.
Hello, my child.
This is your mother
In you inside.

I love you so much.
I wish you just knew
How much it pains me
To see what you went through.

My heart, how it aches
To see you in pain,
To see the same karma
Of me, in you sustain.

I wish you true happiness.
I wish you true peace.
I wish you can heal quick
With GOD and with ease.

There are so many things
That I am wishing to say,
But I know you don't hear me.
So in GOD, I will pray.

I'll tell him I'm sorry
For not being enough,
For not protecting you
When you needed love.

You are my true treasure.
I wish you just knew.
If only I took your pain
And protected you true.

Now is my reckoning
In which I will redeem.
In GOD, I wish to save you.
In him, you will gleam.

Please don't mistake
My wrongdoings in vain.
I also am healing
Through my personal pain.

Together, we can heal.
Together, we'll try.
Together, my child.
Together, we'll fly!

I wish you true blessings.
I wish you true love.
I wish for you happiness
In your spirit in dove.

Please, child, forgive me,
For I know not what I do.
I wish I was better,
To be a mother for you.

But know that I'm trying.
Know that you're blessed.
Know that in our love,
We will pass every test.

TRUE LOVE KNOWS NO BOUNDS

8 OF PENTACLES x QUEEN OF WANDS

The love of a mother
Is not what it seems.
You see all my demons,
But I see all your dreams.

I see your awakening.
I feel your hell.
I feel your struggles.
I see how you fell.

I will never abandon you,
My child, hear me true.
I will always be here
For your children and you.

This is the true power
Of true love in vain.
For a mother's true love
Will endure any pain.

You tell me to leave you,
I will always still stay.
For in GOD we see
There will be a new day.

I wish I could speak to you,
But you do not hear.
I try to reach out,
But you reject me in fear.

Please, my child, hear me.
True love knows no bounds.
I will endure so much pain
Just for you to be found **(by GOD)**.

This is my true calling:
To be there for you,
To heal you from suffering
After what you went through.

Please don't reject me.
Don't close the door.
For in GOD, he promised
That heaven is sure!

Let's go there together.
Let's see, let's just try.
Together, we'll see GOD.
Together, we'll fly!

CONFLICTED IN LOVE

5 OF WANDS

My heart, how it hurts.
How I fear you so much.
I seek to just love you,
But you hate my touch.

Conflict arises,
Confronting in fear.
You fear to be near me.
I know this, my dear.

But know that I'm trying
To amend all my ways,
In all I neglected
In your early days.

If only I knew now
What you needed back then.
I would have been more
Of a mother and friend.

Just know that I love you.
Just know that I'm here.
Just know that in GOD,
No long should we fear.

For in GOD, he promises
To heal all our ways,
To turn our skies blue,
Turn night into day.

We are only human,
And in this I know.
But through GOD's pure love,
Together we'll grow.

I wish you could hear me.
I wish you could see
Everything I do for you
Is to set your heart free!

A MOTHER'S LOVE SUFFERING

THE HERMIT

In silence, I suffer.
In silence, I wait.
In silence, I'm praying.
I wait for my fate.

Please see my true essence.
Please see my true soul.
For all that I wish is
For you to be whole!

My child, how I suffer.
I suffer in vain.
I see all your sins.
I feel all your pain.

For you are my womb.
I still love you like new.
This I know darling.
So in this, I'll be true.

True as a mother,
True in my ways
To be faithful and patient
For a better day.

I know GOD is listening.
I know that he hears.
I know that one day he'll tell you
There is no need to fear.

I am your mother.
I am your soul.
Without forgiveness,
We cannot be whole.

Please see my true colours.
Please hear my true song.
You and your children
Are with me all along.

It is you that I live for.
It is in you I pray
That GOD will redeem you
And bring brighter days.

Please know I will go
To hell and come back
Just to see you and your children
Get back on track.

This is a true mother's love,
One that is pure.
For even in evil,
Our love will endure!

GOD, he is listening.
GOD, he is true.
I know he will bring us
A new day that is blue!

A NEW DAY AWAKENED!

ACE OF WANDS

Hello, my dear mother.
I now hear your cries.
I understand now
Through all of my trials.

Here, you endured suffering.
Here, you endured pain.
Here you stuck by me
And withstood me in vain.

This is now our healing,
For GOD heard your prayers.
He is talking to me now,
Telling me to be fair.

I know I'm not easy,
Yet here you are.
Demons around me.
Battles and scars.

I know you are patient.
I know you are kind.
I know that through GOD's love,
A new world we'll find.

My mother, I'm sorry
For all of your pain.
You suffered in silence
And suffered in vain.

But here, GOD is talking
To me in my cards,
Telling me your story
And how you cry hard.

He hears all your tears.
He sees all your scars.
He sees all your battles.
He hears from afar.

Today, he is healing us.
He is here now to say:
This is our awakening
To a new brighter day!

PSALM 21

TEARS OF EVE
FOR MY SISTERS

25th of May, 2019

THE VOICE OF GOD

THE HIEROPHANT REVERSED

There is a true voice;
The voice deep inside.
There's no need to fear,
No need to hide.

The voice, it does conquer
The evil around.
For this is the word of GOD—
That is the sweet sound.

You must hear this reason,
The voice of true will,
Of GOD in his honesty,
Of love he will fill.

This is the promise
Of GOD: to unite
When you win the battle
And win your fight

We all have our demons.
We all have our sins.
But with GOD, all things possible,
And true love will WIN!

Your heart, it is hurting
Because you are not whole.
But with this true entity,
You will find gold from coal.

GOD, he is merciful.
He hears all your prayers,
Redeems you from suffering
And from all your despairs.

You must listen to reason,
To the voice deep inside.
For this is GOD within you.
There's no need to hide.

He is with you in suffering.
He is with you in toil.
He is with you for miracles
With true love in your coil!

QUEEN OF REDEMPTION

QUEEN OF SWORDS
REVERSED x 4 OF CUPS

The Queen of redemption,
She is here now to stay.
In her, she will guide you
To bring your night into day.

There is a great battle
That lies within us all.
This is the legacy from Eve,
From the wake of our fall.

But GOD, he's now calling
For all of the Queens
Who fell in their suffering
And lost all their dreams.

I am here to guide you.
I am here to say
That GOD is within you;
And in you, he will stay!

The wives of the nightfall,
We all have been marked **(666)**.
But in GOD, we are trusting.
He will give us our arc
(great arcanum, book of life).

Wisdom and knowledge
Is what you must strive.
For many are lost
Who are damned, not alive.

I am here to bring you
To your true self again,
To find your self 'wakened
To your dreams in heaven.

Here I am calling.
I have suffered as you.
But GOD is within us
To turn our skies blue.

Do not cry, my sister.
I am here in your heart
To keep you from falling
And create a new start.

I am but an angel
That was fallen from sin.
But when we turn to GOD,
Our light shines within.

This is a true message
From GOD to tell you
That your true heaven is waiting,
And your skies will turn blue!

YOUR TRUE LOVE AWAKENED

2 OF CUPS REVERSED

Your true love is in you.
It is not in sin **(lust)**.
You must seek the light
That shines truly within.

My heart, it was broken.
It was broken in two.
But now I am whole again
Without residue **(purified)**.

My heart is now whole,
And yours can be too!
For you are a child of GOD,
And I am with you.

Guidance is calling
For you to turn
Your sins to redemption.
In fire, we'll burn.

But do not be worried.
Do not dismay.
All that you've lost
Will return back some day.

GOD will bless you in tenfold.
He will recover your loss.
For you are redeemed
In the stars and the cross.

Magdalene saves us.
She is our true Queen.
For in her, our sins
Will all be redeemed.

She suffered as we did.
But my sister, we passed!
We found the other side
Of the garden and grass
(the grass is greener on the other side).

Love is all around us.
We must seek to find.
For in this, we'll find our soul
When we lose our mind.

My sister, I'm here for you.
Read closely these words:
You are blessed from GOD.
Hear the sweet song and birds!

Garden of Eden,
Our heaven awaits!
Today is your day of waking
To seal your true fate!

UNITED IN SISTERHOOD

4 OF WANDS

United in sisterhood.
United in hands.
We all need each other.
United we stand.

We must help each other,
As I have helped you,
To all turn our skies
To a true colour blue.

Do not be jealous.
Do not harm one's soul.
For we are all broken,
Seeking to all become whole.

We must strive to love.
We must strive to hear
That we all need each other
To redeem us from fear.

We are all broken.
We are all seeking love.
We all have our sins,
But we are redeemed in the dove.

We must hold each other
In times of despair,
For this is true love.
In sisters, we care.

Come together, my sisters.
Today, we unite!
For we'll win the battle
If we hold each other tight.

TEARS OF EVE: FORGIVE ME, MY SISTERS

9 OF SWORDS

My sister, you're crying.
My sister, I hear.
My sister, I feel you.
I sense all your tears.

My sister, I'm sorry
For all that I've done.
I left you in suffering
When we should have been one.

My sister, I love you.
I am sorry, please hear;
I wallowed in pity
And in my own tears.

I fell in my suffering,
And I hurt you, I know.
But today, please forgive me,
And from here we can grow.

I love you regardless.
I love you with heart.
You were there for me
Through my sins from the start.

I wish you real happiness.
I wish you true love.
I am sorry I left you
And stole your true dove.

Please forgive me, my sister.
I love you, it's true.
I am here to ask forgiveness
And turn your skies blue.

Your tears, they will heal soon.
Your pain, it will go.
For in true love, you will wake,
Blossom and grow!

My heart, it is beating.
It is beating for you;
For you to be whole,
Find your dreams and your truth!

THE HEALING POWER: TEARS OF EVE

3 OF SWORDS REVERSED

When Eve, she fell,
She lost her wake.
The devil found her.
Her soul he did take.

But in this suffering,
She did find tears.
The healing power
From all of her fears.

The crystal water,
It showered her sins.
And from this crystal
Showed her true light within.

Her heart, it was mended.
It became one and whole.
For the tears turned to pearls,
Made gold from coal.

The true magic of tears,
The true healing of Eve,
Is the gift from GOD
That we must receive.

There is magic around us.
The love of our pain.
To turn night into day
And remove us from vain.

Eve, she is calling
For you to be one;
To be true and restored,
And create a new SUN!

My sister, I feel you.
I went through the same.
But our tears, they can heal us
From all hurt and pain.

Find your midheaven.
It is waiting for you
To turn every darkness
Into a sky blue.

Tears from our suffering.
Tears from the knife.
But in this, our heart will heal
And bring us new life!

PSALM 22

THE CIRCLE OF LIFE

26th of May, 2019

DEATH IN REVERSE

NEW BEGINNINGS

10 OF SWORDS

For every ending,
There is a beginning.
For every beginning,
There is an end.

This is the
True message.
For GOD,
He will send.

This is the true story
Of Adam and Eve.
This is the true story
That we must believe!

For in every ending,
There is a removal of curse.
It is a new beginning.
It is death in reverse.

Today is your waking
For a new brighter day.
For the demons within you,
You have killed them in slay!

Do not fear darkness,
For I am with you.
In this, you will find
GOD and the truth.

This is the true story
To remove our curse.
The meaning of life
Is death in reverse **(rebirth).**

When you awaken,
You will see a new day.
You will soon find the curse
All fade away.

You will see your true being
Reveal a new light.
For you will see GOD
When you win your fight!

This is absolution
From your curse and your sins.
This is the real fairytale
Where your dreams will begin!

I am within you.
I am your truth.
I am GOD speaking,
And you will see proof!

When you awaken from death,
You will then be blessed.
For you will find Eden
When you pass the test!

REMOVING THE CURSE: BEFORE ENTERING EDEN

THE CHARIOT REVERSED

Stop here, my sister!
Before you can move,
You must find your suffering
And have it removed!

I see all the darkness
Around you and glare.
I see your great curse,
Your pain and despair.

Before you can enter,
Before you can wake,
You must remove all this
And give your soul for the take.

Your soul, it is buried
And covered in sand.
But come here, my sister.
Come hold my hand!

Ride in my chariot.
Let's ride to the clouds,
Find a new world,
The trumpet and sounds.

Hear the sweet birds sing.
Hear the sweet song.
Your light is within you.
It was there all along!

Find your true light, dear,
And remove the great curse.
For the new world awaiting
In a new Universe.

The chariot waiting.
Let's ride to our death.
For we will find new life
When we take our last breath.

Rebirth is calling
For us to unite **(with GOD),**
Find our true higher selves,
And find our true sight!

JUDGEMENT DAY

7 OF SWORDS x JUDGEMENT

This is your judgement.
This is your time.
This is when you will meet
The great DIVINE.

You will wake in glory!
You will see a new day!
You will realise your power,
For the beast you did slay!

I am here for you, sister.
I am here by your side,
Waving the red flag.
There's no need to hide!

You are now awakened.
You are now redeemed.
Everything you thought you lost
Is not what it seemed.

Today, you are saved.
Today, you are crowned.
Today, you found GOD
Through the trumpets and sound.

Awaken, my sister!
The skies are so blue.
Today is your day.
Today is your truth!

Judgement is calling
For you to be saved.
Hear the sweet angels.
Create a new day.

Angels of fallen,
I am with you.
Phoenix of ashes,
You can walk on through.

The gates, they are opening,
Flooding your heart,
Awakening your truth,
Revealing new start.

Come in, my sister.
The grass is so green!
Look at the garden.
It's so serene!

Kingdom of heaven,
O' how it is true!
The grass is so green,
And the skies are so blue.

Find here, your happiness.
Find here, your truth.
Reveal your true destiny.
Reveal your true youth!

THE EMPRESS REDEEMED

THE EMPRESS REVERSED

The empress redeemed.
The empress rebirth.
The empress and mother
Of heaven and earth.

Here you are, finally!
Here you are crowned.
Here you are, home again.
You were lost, now you're found.

Empress, you're glowing.
Empress, your light!
Empress, your crystal
Reveals your true sight.

O' what an honour.
Empress, you're crowned!
I see your gifts
And hear your sweet sound.

O' Empress, you're honoured.
This is your true home.
In your true element,
On your real throne.

Empress, you're twinkling.
Empress, your gleam!
Empress, you're shining
With a true light and beam.

Your heart, it is bright.
It is the new SUN—
Revealing true youth,
Uniting as one.

Finding you honoured,
It humbles my soul.
For now I can see
You are finally whole!

FINDING YOUR TRUTH, FINDING YOUR LIGHT

9 OF CUPS REVERSED

We all have our truth.
We all have our light.
We all have our woes
That came from the fight.

But my dear, let me tell you:
This curse is a gift.
Find your true happiness
When you are able to shift!

Energies moving,
High and low tides.
But when you awaken,
It will reveal a new side.

You will find your truth
Was hiding in curse.
For the gifts that reveal themselves
Are rich and diverse.

You will find true melody.
You will find your song.
You will find creation.
It was there all along.

You will become GOD,
For GOD is just love.
And in love, you create
Through your spirit and dove.

Your gifts, they will heal you
And show your real truth.
In this, you will find
Abundance and youth.

No long will you hide
From the evil around,
For this will create your
Art and your sound.

True magic awaits
To reveal your light.
Remove the veil,
Revealing true sight.

We are all true beings
With magic around.
We all have a sweet song
Alchemised in our sound.

Find your true melody.
Find yourself crowned.
Truth and light waiting
When love is around!

THE GREAT DEBATE

2 OF PENTACLES REVERSED

There is a great battle
Of good and of bad.
There is a dichotomy
Of happy and sad.

There are two shadows,
For we are all dual.
But what we must find
Is to use this as fuel!

We are all but energy.
We are all but light;
Looking to reveal ourselves
From the shadows at night.

We must know our battle
And speak out our truth.
For in this, we will find
That GOD is our proof...

Proof that the light
Will brighten our day.
Proof that our shadows
Do not have to stay.

We must work in harmony
To master our truth.
For this will reveal itself
When GOD is our proof!

PSALM 23

VIRTUES IN WAKE THE BATTLE OF GOOD AND EVIL

27th of May, 2019

THE GREAT DEBATE

THE LOVERS

There is a decision
That you need to make:
Will you go back to sleep
Or will you stay in wake?

This is the great question
That GOD's asking you:
If you will to be whole again
Or stay broken in two.

There are so many entities
That wish for your fall,
But you have redeemed yourself.
You must truly stand tall!

The lovers card lives
As the card of debate.
It asks you to follow
Your dreams and your fate.

Do not be swayed
By the forces outside.
Wounded healer, my angel,
You must remove pride
(ego, fear)!

If you feel you are falling,
Just look back within.
Ask GOD to redeem you
From your suffering.

I know you are hurting
Each time you do heal.
The vampires around you,
Your energy they steal.

They see your great aura,
And they wish for this too.
But my dear, you're a healer.
This was fated for you.

You must know your **power**
Exists in your mind.
To overcome obstacles
And use it to grind!

Use your great power
For your art and your work.
Use it for energy.
Good or bad, still a perk.

You must know your north node,
Your ARIES, awaits!
This is your true destiny—
Chiron in your fate
(May is Chiron in ARIES).

Wounded healer, I feel for you.
For this role can be hard.
You may feel defeated,
But stand tall. Don't stay scarred.

Use your true pain
To move to north node.
For this will invoke you
To use all of the codes
(clues, symbols from GOD).

Use them in prayer.
Use them in space.
Use them to strengthen you
In the evil you face.

There are many willing
To see you again fall.
But in this, you must realise—
In evil, stand tall!

You are a true saint
Redeemed in the light.
You must keep your virtues
In the great battle and fight!

Remove all your weaknesses
And turn them to strengths.
Remove all your vices,
And you will regain lengths.

Lengths in endurance.
Lengths in your path.
Lengths on your journey
With your ROD and your staff
(Psalm 23:4 NIV).

This is your GOD calling
For you to stand tall!
For you must save many
From the wake of the fall.

Move closer to destiny
And use your virtues.
Take all that could destroy you
As energy you can use.

Pray to the GODS
That they will guide you.
For this path, it is long.
But with GOD, you'll be true!

BALANCING VIRTUES

6 OF PENTACLES x 3 OF WANDS

There is a great destiny
That lies here for you.
It is to help others
And bring them to truth.

Hard as it seems,
You are fated in vow.
You must know your calling.
On your path, it is now.

You must help others,
And it starts with your home.
Your mother, she's tainted.
With the devil, she's grown.

You must know your calling
Is to help others redeem.
For the virtues you hold
Is the light you must beam!

Use all you can
In your heart and your mind
For those who are seeking,
That do wish to find.

You have a great calling
As a message from GOD:
To lead with the book of life,
With your staff and your ROD.

Go forth in virtue,
And you must truly stand tall.
For you are the one
Who will help save lost souls.

The ending is coming,
And many they fear.
But when you give guidance,
GOD's voice they will hear.

You must use your virtues
In the face of distress.
For this is your shield.
And in this, you'll be blessed.

Do not fear the entities
That do surround you.
For GOD, he is on your side
With intention and truth.

Go forth as fearless **(soul).**
You must not retreat.
For the road, it is long.
Do not bow down to defeat.

Use all that destroys you,
And rise up with strength!
For your journey's just started
In time and in length.

Do not be tainted.
You must keep your vow.
For this is GOD telling you
To move forward fearlessly now!

LEADER OF THE NEW WORLD

6 OF WANDS REVERSED

There is a great calling
That I have for you.
In this, you must strive
To stay loyal and true.

Leader of the new world,
Your Heaven awaits!
The battle is long.
But your path, it is fate.

You must share your stories,
And you must do this now.
This is part of your calling
And part of your vow.

Do not fear or worry,
For GOD is within you.
You must move to the new world
That is waiting anew.

Leader of the new world,
I know you are strong.
Your virtues, they've lasted
Through evil and wrong.

Know this is destined;
You cannot escape.
For your very existence is
To create new landscape.

Move forward, my dearest.
Keep fighting each day.
Your ARIES within you
Will assist you to slay!

There's evil around you,
But you must not retreat!
For in you, GOD wills
For you to win in defeat!

Leader of the new world,
Use your virtues in wake.
For your reward, it is many.
A new world for the take!

ATTACHMENT AND SUFFERANCE

THE DEVIL

The devil had taken you.
He saw your great needs.
He lured you and tempted you.
And then, you found greed.

You must hold your virtues
In the face of such tempt.
For the ones that are luring you
Are the ones who are unkempt **(unclean).**

You will know they are tainted
And they are with sin.
For their dishevelled appearance
Will show no GOD within.

For the ones who hold virtue,
They are clean and are bright.
They hold true life spirit
And shine bright in the night.

You will know the devil
When he crosses your path.
He hides in attachment
And true sociopaths.

The ones who are holding you
Are the ones with much sin.
For they hold you in suffering
And with the DEVIL within.

Attachment they use
To tempt you to fall.
For they give you things,
But expect you to crawl **(belittle yourself, beg).**

Know your true virtues
To stand and stay wake.
For the devil around you,
You must slay with a stake.

Remove them from holding you.
Remove them from seed.
In this, GOD will guide you.
You must take true heed!

They pretend to be helpers
When they are of taint.
You must know your virtues
And stay true as a saint!

Do not be pulled to them.
You must use your force!
For you are with power.
For you are with Source!

REMOVING ATTACHMENTS IN KARMIC DEBT

JUSTICE REVERSED

My dear, you must balance
Your virtues from vice.
You must look at your energy
And hold your strength thrice
(united with GOD and spirit).

The devil is trying
To take you again.
But in this, hold your sword
And keep it sharpened!

Use your true power
And use your true force.
Remove all your sufferance
And all your discourse.

My dear, use your fire.
ARIES in you, you must feel.
For this is your destiny.
In GOD, you are sealed.

You must hold your virtues.
You must stand truly tall!
For you will conquer,
Be redeemed from your fall.

The devil awaits you.
He is waiting your heed.
Do not reduce yourself
To vice or to greed.

Remove all attachments
From others. Don't take;
For this is what will give you
A new life in wake!

Give back attachments
To the ones who lure you.
For this will keep you
Solemn and true.

You must thank them dearly
For their pretend help in wealth.
For this will invoke you
To fend for yourself!

You must know that people
Have agendas for you.
They wish for your powers
And keep you attached just like glue.

Remove your attachments
And you will be free.
This will be the true path
To your new destiny.

Work hard in waking.
Work hard for your fate **(goal attainment).**
For this is your destiny.
Your new world awaits!

RESTORING BALANCE: THE GREAT BATTLE IS WON!

JUSTICE

My dear, you have made it!
You've passed the great test.
You've defeated your fears,
And now you are blessed.

This was the great sufferance
That you had endured
In hiding from your fears.
But now, you are cured!

You held up your sword
And straightened your crown.
Now you are balanced
And the devil bows down.

You have conquered your beasts
And the devil within.
For now you have overcome
Fear and great sin!

I am so proud of you,
My angel, my child,
For you attained victory
Of your mind going wild!

Just know that in **excellence,**
You must strive for each day.
For this is in **habit,**
And in GOD you should pray!

Wake with intention.
Wake with true sight.
Wake with your sword
To keep for your battle and fight.

The ones who attract to you
Have the devil within.
It is your duty and honour
To remove them of sin.

Be strong here, my child,
For there are further tests.
But in being aware,
You will conquer the rest!

Mastery, it is calling
For you, Queen of kings,
To become your true highest **(self)**
And defeat your surroundings.

True victory in you.
I do see virtues.
For you are so brave.
For in GOD, you did choose!

This battle is over.
Your soul is restored.
But keep open your eye,
For the battles are more.

Just know, in your virtues,
You will remove fear.
Keep on the path ahead,
And in GOD you'll stay clear.

Keep solid around you
Your version of truth.
For your purpose and mission
Is in GOD and your youth **(children).**

Your future is plenty.
Your gifts, they do wake!
For your virtues have saved you
From the fear that is fake.

Choose wisely each day.
For in decisions, you'll win!
Choose GOD over suffering,
And you will conquer sin.

My child, you are blessed.
Your soul, it is true.
For you have picked GOD
And held your virtues!

PSALM 24

YOUR WORD, YOUR WAY!

28th of May, 2019

YOU ARE ONE WITH GOD!

6 OF PENTACLES

You are a child,
A child of GOD.
You are the life.
You are the ROD!

Do you not see
That you are the one?
No need to fear.
For in love, you've won!

Every day you wake,
You must give your praise **(gratitude).**
For in GOD, all things possible
With new life and new day.

My dear, I am with joy!
I am so very pleased.
You have found power
And create life now with ease.

GOD is within you,
You now live your dreams!
Do you not feel the warmth?
Do you not feel your gleam?

You are brighter than day.
You are higher than life!
For you are with GOD,
United as wife.

Do you not see
That the vow is within,
Not with a man
Or reduction to sin?

You are so beautiful.
If only you knew
That GOD wills you to win
And be yourself true!

My heart, it is full
And beating for you
To find in you true love
And be whole from two.

Merging your energies.
Merging your mind.
You are now one with GOD
In space and in time!

LIVING YOUR DREAM!!!

5 OF PENTACLES REVERSED
x 2 OF CUPS

Abundance in dreams.
My dear, you're awake!!!
I am so happy for you.
Claimed your soul for the take!

You are one with GOD.
You are living your truth,
Restoring your EDEN
And finding your youth **(in the cup of life).**

My dear, you are glistening.
You are a true star!
Claiming your dreams;
It no longer seems far.

UNITED as one! *Casal*
Female CHRIST is your SEED. *Krista*
Rising from Ashes.
Reborn and living your dreams! *Phoenix*

My dear, you're a vision—
True beauty in sight!
You are one with GOD.
In CHRIST, you unite.

I love you, my child.
You are loyal and true.
You have found your strength
From being broken in two.

You pushed through the odds.
You conquered your fears.
Now you are one,
And your dreams, they are clear.

The truth you did seek,
And the truth you did find.
Now you are one
In spirit and mind
(uniting chakras and energies).

My daughter of Christ,
I now see your wings!
Live in your dreams.
In this new life, you will sing!

YOUR TRUTH AND YOUR LIGHT!

6 OF CUPS

Your truth and your light.
Your children, your womb.
Your reason for breathing.
Your flowers in bloom!

Your children, your legacy.
Your children, your health.
Your children, your blessings.
Your children, your wealth.

True GOD is within you,
For you know only of love.
Your children recover you.
They are your true doves.

Your life, it is gleaming.
The moon and the sun
Both merged together,
Together as one!

Your children, your gifts,
Pure essence and light.
Giving your soul back,
Recovering sight.

True living in honour
For your children and soul
That give you true meaning,
Bringing you back to whole!

SING YOUR TRUE SONG!

ACE OF PENTACLES

Your song is your gold,
Your vision and sight.
Your song is your truth,
Your day and your night.

Do you hear the sweet melody
In your voice? It is clear.
For your gold in abundance,
It is here, it is near.

Your life is your testimony
Of GOD and your gifts.
In this, you will rise
And sing from the cliffs!

Rise, my true angel.
Sing your sweet song!
For your gifts, they were there
In you all along,

Your life is a blessing,
And you are a dream.
In this, you will 'waken.
In this, you will gleam!

Star seed awakened.
Star seed of light!
Sing your sweet melody.
Shine love! Shine bright!

Sing of your love.
Sing of your truth.
Sing your true melody.
Sing of your youth!

My dear, this is your gift,
For you have stayed true.
You have stayed loyal
To GOD in virtue.

Keep focused on life.
Keep focused on love.
Your true sun inside you.
Your song is your dove!

VICTORIOUS DREAMS!

ACE OF SWORDS

Victory calling!
Victory clear.
Victory with you.
Victory near.

My child, you are honoured,
Anointed by seed.
You will bring true light
And give love in need.

You are a true vision,
True beauty in sight.
You are alpha, omega.
You are pure in your light.

GOD, he is willing
For you to attest,
To give His name in true victory.
In this, you are blessed!

You must speak your truth.
You must light the way
For the ones who need you
To bring a new day.

You must sing in honour.
You must sing in praise.
For you will show GOD
And light the true way.

My dear, they are calling.
They are calling for you
To bring them the light
And show them anew **(a new life).**

PSALM 25

FIND YOUR VIRTUES!

29ᵗʰ of May 2019

HUMILITY IS VICTORY

JUSTICE x 5 OF SWORDS REVERSED

Humility is victory.
This is real virtue.
For the ones around you
Will you to lose.

When you come across others,
Do not act to defeat.
Instead, act in harmony
And take the back seat.

Allow them to attack you.
You must concede.
For this is not your battle.
You must take GOD's heed.

You are just a mirror **(twin flame)**
That shows them their sin;
To teach them a lesson,
To find their own light within.

My dear, it is hard.
I know this is true.
But in this, you will find
Yourself strong in virtue!

It will strengthen your will
And your way without taint.
This is what will drive you
To stay truly a saint.

For the ones who are humble
Are the ones who are meek.
They are the ones blessed;
For in GOD, they did seek.

Do not be dismayed
For the ones who attack.
For they have their own battle.
You must retreat and stay back.

True honour and victory,
It lies in this test:
To be humble from ego,
Set you apart from the rest!

DILIGENCE IN REBIRTH

8 OF PENTACLES x THE EMPRESS

There is a great virtue
That you hold deep inside.
It removes all your ego
And swallows your pride.

It stands test of time
And knows no defeat.
It is the virtue of diligence—
Staying true in retreat.

You must stay in solitude
To perfect your true skills.
For your gifts and your craft
Are developed through will.

You must be diligent
In your tasks and affairs.
For this will remove you
From all the false glares **(evil eyes, negativity).**

For in diligence, you strive
To become your own best.
You remove jealous eyes
And you pass your own test.

You do not focus on others,
For you are with soul.
In diligence and perfection,
You will stay true and whole.

You must know your gifts.
They are rare without taint.
For this is the true virtues
Given to saints!

Your gift of intelligence.
Your gift of great song.
Your gift of great virtues.
It was there all along!

You must strengthen your will
And your word and your way.
For this will redeem you
In virtue each day.

Find your true light.
It is in diligent toil.
For this will create your land
And nurture your soil.

Find your true midheaven.
This victory, it awaits.
For this is your good fortune.
This is your true fate!

PATIENCE IS A VIRTUE

9 OF CUPS REVERSED

You start many projects,
But then you have failed.
But do not dismay.
For every night, there is day.

You will find your virtues
When you pass this true test:
To defy all the odds.
In this, you'll be blessed.

Do not worry for failure,
For this is not true defeat.
You must dust your shoulders
And get back on your feet.

Recover from failure,
For this is the test:
To be patient and willing,
To first recover and rest.

You are with true gifts,
But you must nurture them so.
Patience is needed.
In this, you will grow.

You must recover from failure
And get back to the grind.
For you must nurture your skills
And nurture your mind.

Stay true to your calling,
Stay true on your path,
Be patient in virtue
And develop your craft.

You must know your weakness
To turn it to strength.
This is true patience
In time and in length.

Know now your lessons
From failure are true.
For they will develop
Yourself in virtue!

CURSE IN REVERSE

8 OF SWORDS REVERSED

There is a real sickness
That exists in this world.
There are many suffering.
In this, you must learn.

The battle around us
Is not our own fight.
Everyone has their demons.
In this, know your true sight!

You must know projection
When it is aimed toward you.
For everyone suffers
From being broken in two.

You must know their demons,
But you must know yours first.
For this will remove you from sin
And turn the curse in reverse.

For curses are nothing
But spells in blindsight.
But when you remove yourself,
You will conquer the fight.

Know that the battle
Exists for us all.
Do not reduce yourself
To others' battles and fall.

This will truly set you
Apart from the rest.
For in this reversal of curse,
You will pass every test.

You must know your weakness.
You must know your vice.
You must know your suffering.
In this, pray to be thrice
(one with GOD and spirit).

This will remove you
From the true suffering
That is the curse of others,
And create a buffering.

Your light is your shield.
Turn a curse in reverse.
For this will redeem you
From others' bad curse.

You will know you suffer
If you engage in their sin.
For in this, you will feel
A great battle within.

You must bless those who curse you
And concede to them; bow.
For this will redeem you
And keep you in your true vow
(To GOD and purity)!

QUEEN OF VIRTUE, QUEEN OF LIGHT

QUEEN OF PENTACLES

Queen of virtue.
Queen of light.
Queen of redemption.
Queen of the night.

Queen, you are blessed.
Queen, you are whole.
Queen, you are humble.
You create gold from coal.

Queen, you are virtuous.
Queen, you are blessed.
Queen, you have passed
Every one of GOD's tests.

Queen, you are diligent,
Patient and kind.
Queen, you are focused
In leading the blind.

Queen of true love.
Queen of true life.
Queen, you redeem us all
From sin and from strife.

Queen, you inspire.
Queen, you are bright.
Queen, you are truly
With GOD in this fight.

Queen, please save us
From our sins and ourselves.
Teach us your virtues.
Teach us to mend.

Queen, please show us
The light and the way.
For we need to recover
From the beast. Help us slay!

Queen, you are strong
Yet beautiful and fair.
Queen, with true vision
You remove all false glares **(evil eye).**

Queen, you are honoured.
Queen, you are true.
Please help us find GOD
And bring our world to anew!

REVEALING YOUR MOON

THE MOON

In finding your truth,
You must find your moon.
Shine it with honour.
In this, GOD will swoon.

We all have our demons.
We all have our night.
But in our new moon,
We will shine so bright.

For when we find peace
In our darkness, despair,
This will remove our sins
When we are able to share.

We must recover our honour.
We must be patient and kind.
For the battle within us
Requires WILL of the mind
(willpower, mind over matter).

We cannot move forward
If we cannot reveal.
For in this, we'll still suffer.
No long can we heal.

We all have a sun side.
We all have our moon.
But in revealing our shadows,
We will turn night into noon.

We will show our true placements
Exists in our sun.
And in merging these energies,
We will become one.

We are wives of nightfall.
We all have our sins.
But in this, we must reveal
And shine the true light within!

PSALM 26

GOD'S PROMISE IN FAITH! A PURE SEED

30th of May 2019

GOD'S PROMISE IN FAITH!

ACE OF PENTACLES

Hear ye, my child!
The Kingdom from faith.
You have conquered your shadows
And lasted the wait!

You are shining so bright.
I can see light within!
You are truly magnificent.
In LOVE, you did win!

My child, you're a star!
You are now in the sky,
Waiting to shoot.
Now you can fly!

GOD's promise in faith.
GOD's promise is true:
To bring you new life
And real gifts for you!

You are with abundance.
You are with pure joy.
Your gift of obedience
Is a child; a new boy!

I will give you your treasures.
I will give you true gold.
I will give you your blessings.
You will never grow old.

You will find your true vessels
Of CHRIST are in blood.
Your children of royalty,
Gifted from GOD!

This is GOD's promise:
To answer your prayers,
To keep you sealed and pure,
And keep you in care!

My dear, you are beautiful.
You are chosen through faith.
Live your real dreams now.
This is your true fate!

NEW LIFE, TRUE VESSELS!

(MESSENGERS OF GOD)
KING OF SWORDS x THE FOOL

My dear, the SUN,
How it shines in your face!
You now know your purpose.
You now know your place!

Take your true seating
On the thrown with your crown.
Here you will glisten,
And they will all bow down.

Seeing your purpose.
Seeing your light.
Seeing your purity
Truly shine bright!

Your song is a vessel
In which they will hear GOD.
You will give them the truth
In your vessel and blood.

Your children of purity—
How they are your truth,
Your legacy and future
Presented in youth.

Your bloodline awaits you,
The royal and pure.
This was your true destiny,
So clean and demure.

Your children, your bloodline,
Your legacy awaits!
Handing down your teachings,
Creating new faith.

Your teachings from GOD,
O' how they are real.
Your children, your legacy,
The vessels revealed!

DARK ANGEL AWAKENED!

TEMPERANCE

Awakened dark angel,
How you are blessed!
Coming from darkness,
Yet passed every test!

Shining through turmoil,
Rising through sin,
Cleansing your waters
With your true light within.

You see the explosions.
The old world, it fades—
Banishing darkness,
Creating new days.

My dear, you are gifted,
Anointed through GOD.
You must lead the others
With your fist and your ROD.

Do you hear the bells ringing?
Your third eye, shining real.
You must give out the book of life
To truly reveal!

This is your true mission,
GOD's new book of life.
To set it in corners
And save women from strife.

The old world is ending.
A new world awaits.
You must go forth in mission.
You can no longer wait!

This is an emergency.
The bells ringing in ears!
Many women are fading.
You must cleanse their tears.

Shine your true beauty.
Shine your true light!
Dark angel awakened,
Come out from the night!!!

This is GOD speaking.
Do I need to shout?
Do not hide any longer.
You must truly come out!!!

Reveal your true beauty.
Reveal your true light.
Reveal your true legacy,
For you are a TRUE SIGHT!

BROKEN DREAMS, NEW FAITH

8 OF SWORDS

Your heart, it was broken
And torn at the seam.
You felt you failed in life.
Broken life, broken dreams.

Your heart, it was crying,
But your past love did not hear.
For he was in his own suffering
And in his own fears.

But this is GOD's promise
That He has for you:
No long will you be broken
Or torn still in two.

You have a new chance now.
Your Chiron is back
To teach you some lessons
And get you back on track.

Your new life is waiting—
Your children, your faith—
To present you new days.
Your new life awaits!

My dear, you will regain
All that you lost.
For you endured suffering,
But redeemed through the cross.

You will create a new life.
You will have a new home.
You will secure your true loves
And make your own throne!

You do not need mortal man
When GOD is with you.
For this will secure you
And bring you back to anew.

You will gain all the strength
And the courage you need
To secure your new life
By taking GOD's heed.

Do not be fearful.
A new life awaits!
For this is GOD's promise
When you live in faith!

GOD'S PROMISE TO YOU!

THE LOVERS REVERSED

**(Tone Stith, This Woman's Work -
Maxwell Tribute)**

A new day awakened.
A promise of faith!
My child, do not fear,
For this is your true fate!

To be the true woman
That your children will see;
That they wish to emulate,
That they wish to be!

You have so much strength in you.
You have to shine bright!
Do not let the torment of life
Dim your true light.

You are a strong woman.
In this, I know true.
For you were blessed from seed
(mother's name Blessie - Blessed Seed).
This is GOD's word to you!

Your life had been broken,
But a new world awaits;
One where you will truly live
In your real dreams and fate.

Garden of Eden—
Can you see all the trees,
The beautiful flowers,
The beautiful breeze?

Your life will be perfect
As you now truly unite
With GOD and your spirit,
And find your true light.

This is GOD speaking to you.
This is the great reveal:
That a new world is waiting.
And in this, you will heal!

This is GOD's promise now,
GOD's promise to you:
That I will show you a new sky
That is truly so blue!

(A PURE CHILD, INDIGO BLUE SKY)

IMMORTAL SEED

4 OF SWORDS REVERSED

There is a prophecy
That I have for you:
You are with child
Named INDIGO BLUE.

This child is the vessel,
The vessel from GOD,
In which he will lead
With an iron fist and ROD.

I know you are scared.
But my dear, this is true.
Your new child from GOD,
INDIGO BLUE.

This child, he is pure.
He is created from seed.
No taint or sufferance.
He will be a new breed.

Immortal, he is
Your vessel, your blood.
DNA of pure Christ seed,
Gifted from GOD.

You are with child.
My dear, please stay pure.
For this child is the wake
Of a new world; the cure.

Enlightened in promise,
Gifted through faith.
You must know this destiny.
It was always your fate!

You must know this prophecy.
It will be revealed.
And from this, you will know
Your fate; it is sealed.

Keep yourself chaste
And keep yourself out of sight.
For when you give birth,
This child will shine bright.

You must not fear this.
You must stay in love **(with your seeds).**
For this is your gift from GOD.
Your message and dove.

Upon his birth, you will cease.
But you will be brought back anew.
Because this child is immortal—
INDIGO BLUE
(Revelation 12:5 NIV).

PSALM 27

BLESSINGS FROM OUR CURSE
SHADOW WORK

31ˢᵗ of May, 2019

UNVEILING THE CURSE

THE LOVERS REVERSED

Unveiling the curse
Is the lovers reversed.
It is finding your demons
That hide in your thirst **(wine)**.

Your thirst in emotions.
Your thirst to express.
You must know that darkness
Is part of the test.

If you wish to unveil this,
You must know this true.
You must find your outlet
To bring you back to anew.

Some may fall to addiction.
Some may fall to the vice.
But you must be strong
And pray to be thrice
(strong, one with GOD and spirit).

In this, you will alchemise.
In this, you will heal.
In this, you will utilise
Your gifts in reveal!

You must use emotion.
You must use your curse.
For this is the lesson
In the lovers reversed.

For the lovers reversed
Is a card of advice.
It is telling you to seek GOD **(your higher self)**
Instead of your vice.

For we are all sinners—
This is the real truth.
For we were banished from Eden
From the beginning of youth **(beginning of time).**

So we must know our darkness.
We must know our sin.
We must know our weaknesses
So we can shine light within.

Unveiling our weakness
Is unveiling our curse.
In this, we will be free
Through the lovers reversed!

WIN THE BATTLE WITHIN!

9 OF PENTACLES x 5 OF WANDS

There is a great weakness
That you must know is true:
The battle of darkness
That lives within you.

We all have our demons.
We all have our vice.
But what we must seek
Is to be with GOD in advice.

"Seek ye the Kingdom"
Is what Bible says;
But it's harder to do
If you are not with prayer.

You must know your shadows,
And you must hold them strong.
You must turn them to gold
So you can turn right from wrong.

Alchemy healing
Will be your best friend;
For in this true skill,
You will learn how to mend.

You must know the weakness
Of the battle within.
For each of us suffer
With the seed of such sin.

We are all born from darkness.
But in this, we find light
From finding our shadows,
Turning day from our night.

The secrets we hold
Are our demons in dark,
For we all hide our shadows.
But when they hide, they do lark
(want to emerge as the beast).

So what we must do then
Is seek our battle within.
From this, we can channel.
And from this, we will win!

Shadow work is our calling
For us to unite.
In merging angel with demon,
We move to day from our night.

We must know this skill
To reveal original sin **(666).**
For in wisdom and virtue,
We will win the battle within!

JUSTICE IS SEALED!

JUSTICE REVERSED

There is a great lesson
In this calling of life:
It is to find our shadow
And redeem our own strife.

This is the great lesson
That we must pass in true test.
For in this will of Ma'at **(Goddess),**
We'll turn cursed to blessed.

The balance of harmony
Is tipped on our scales.
We must know our shadows
So that justice prevails!

For the one who is honest
Is living well in their truth.
In this, you hold victory.
And in this, you'll know youth **(immortality).**

We are all just human.
But in this, it's revealed:
We must tip the balance scales
So that justice is sealed!

We must outweigh our demons.
We must know our curse.
For this is the truest lesson
Of justice reversed!

SHADOWS IN THE DARK!

8 OF CUPS

Shadows lurking in the dark—
They come back every **(full)** moon.
In this, we must find outlet
So we can become immune!

The cup, it gives us solace
To redeem our very sin.
For in this cup of wine,
We will find shadow within.

Shadow work is needed
To find our truth and light.
For if we hide our shadows,
Our demon will come out to fight!

We must absolve the shadows
In the cup of wine within
So we can absolve and alchemise
At the very seed of sin **(before it manifests).**

But in this, we must know something
That is certain and is true:
We must not fall into vice,
For this will break us back to two.

We must be truthful of our shadows
So we can reveal our light.
In this, we will remove the curse
At very seed of sight!

Release the energy within you
That is trapped at root of coil.
For this will cultivate your harvest
And make sure you have right soil
(planting the right seeds in mind).

You must absolve your sinful ways
In wisdom from the arc
(great arcanum, book of life);
In this, you will find freedom
From your shadows in the dark!

REVEALING OUR TRUTH FROM CURSE

TEMPERANCE REVERSED

We are all our own worst enemy,
For we harbour it within.
This is the beast that's talked about,
Marked as original sin **(666)**
(Revelation 13:1 NIV).

We must find our true light calling
After we drink the cup of life.
For we will remove the 6 with scorn
And remove our very strife.

Tell the truth by **absolving.**
Tell your truth and pray.
For in this repentance, we will burn
Our sinful scornful ways.

The purity of water
Is found in cup of wine.
For in this cup, you will alchemise
Your true nature in divine.

Do not be fooled by sin and scorn,
For we are all marked with the beast.
But in this truth, we will reveal
Our shadows through high priest **('ess)**
(higher selves).

This is the truest meaning
Of temperance in reverse.
It is a tale of **absolving**
To reveal our truth from curse!

TO BE MARKED IS THE TEST!

REVELATION 13
4 OF PENTACLES REVERSED

There is a great lesson
We have not learned in defeat.
It is in **Revelation (13:18 NIV),**
About the mark of beast **(666).**

We do not know the meaning
Is there between the lines,
Telling us to reveal our truth
So we can become divine!

We all are sins in shadows
Hiding in the dark.
But in this, we must find wisdom
In the book of life— the ARC.

The ones who judge are hiding.
They are real sinners in the dark.
For they have not found freedom
Through the lines found in the ARC
(book of life, great arcanum).

To be marked is a true blessing,
A blessing in disguise.
For this will reveal your true self,
And no longer will you hide!

To be marked is true freedom,
But to be marked is the true test.
For this is the lesson we must learn
To become our very best!

We cannot know true freedom
If we do not do our shadow work.
For in this, we will not find coin.
For the demons will still lurk
(Revelation 13:16-18 NIV).

This is the truest meaning
Of **4 OF PENTACLES REVERSED.**
For this is telling you to absolve yourself
From seven deadly sins and curse!

444

PSALM 28

DETACHMENT WITH LOVE

31ˢᵗ of May, 2019

LEAVING THE NEST

6 OF SWORDS REVERSED

There is a truth
That we must all come to know;
That is the real secret
In how we can grow.

It lies in detachment
And withdrawal from seed;
From the one you call mother
Who gives you your needs.

There is a time coming
In which you must know this test
Is to remove yourself unconditionally
And leave mother's nest.

For there is a great calling
That is within us all.
But to move to our truest self,
We must heed the great call!

We must stand independent
On our own two strong feet,
So we will find our own destiny
And conquer mother's defeat.

You cannot do this
If mother has pride.
For this will diminish you
And make you lose sight.

You must know your honour
And detach from her, smooth.
To discover a new world
And find your real truth.

There is a great lesson
That lies in us all;
It is the suffering of attachment
That will result in our fall.

Although mother grooms us,
She teaches her ways.
We must know in rebirth.
We must find a new day.

We must unlearn all things
That she has instilled.
For the instillment of some **(mothers)**
Will bind your free will.

This is your great virtue.
This is your great test:
To detach yourself in kind love
Without mother's detest!

FIND YOUR OWN FAMILY!

THE EMPRESS REVEALED!
10 OF CUPS x THE EMPRESS

Find your own family.
Find your fate sealed.
In this, you will find your truth
As the empress revealed!

In becoming your own mother,
You will pass every test.
You will become your own woman
And leave mother's nest.

No long will you be in curse,
For you will create your own way
To make a new family
And create a new day!

The empress is now revealed,
And this is your truth:
You will be discovered soon,
And be the one who bears youth.

The twelve stars, they shine on you.
They twinkle in sun.
For you are now whole again,
And your family is one!

Soon you will come anew,
For you are with child.
You will make a true happy home
And create it with pride.

A new life, it waits for you.
Your Eden in sight.
For you honour your true virtue
As a mother of light!

Your children will cherish you.
You will give them real love.
For you are the truest sun
That shines from above!

PSALM 29

THE SUN!

31st of May, 2019

T H E   S U N !

THE SUN

The sun, it is out!
The sun, it is mine!
The sun, it is glistening
Through space and in time.

The sun is my life.
The sun is my truth.
The sun reveals my flowers
From their seed into bloom.

The sun is my heir.
The sun is my womb.
The sun is my seed
Turning into full bloom.

My children of prophecy.
My children of youth.
My children of purity.
My children of truth!

My children, my gifts from GOD.
My children, my light!
My children from purity
Turning day from my night.

The sun, how it's gleaming.
The sun, how it's pure!
The sun, how it's shining
So bright and demure.

My flowers of optimism.
My true rays of light.
My children of prophecy,
You will shine so bright!

QUEEN OF LIFE

QUEEN OF PENTACLES
REVERSED x ACE OF WANDS

My beautiful Queen,
My angel of light.
The woman of redemption
Recovered from fight.

This is your true beauty.
This is your true song:
To reveal what was inside you
That was there all along!

Find your true freedom.
It lies in your gifts.
The voice of GOD within you,
The voice that will lift!

Sing your true melody.
Sing your true song.
You are so beautiful!
We've waited so long!

GOD is within you,
And in this you are blessed!
A true sun in the sky,
Becoming your best!

Shine like a diamond.
Beam your true rays!
Shine your warm love on me
And brighten my day!

This is your creation
Making light from the dark.
Bring your true song to life,
Your wisdom and arc **(Book of life).**

My Queen, you are glistening.
You have blossomed in youth.
Queen of life, shine your rays on us
And bring us the truth!

MESSAGE OF TRUTH
IN INDIGO BLUE

KNIGHT OF PENTACLES REVERSED

There is a new message
Revealed now to you:
You have further gifts
To bring to anew.

As you dig deeper into the arc,
You find many clues.
This is another revelation
For INDIGO BLUE.

Your son, he will be the truth,
The message from GOD.
He will bring about peace and love,
Removing facades.

He will be a golden child
Beaming with rays.
From his very inception,
Your EDEN will stay!

This is the true gift from GOD
Discovered in you.
The miracle of immaculate
Is INDIGO BLUE.

The cause of your true rebirth,
Discovered in death.
But in this, you will be the truth.
For you will renew in true health.

Ceased you will be for three days,
But come back to youth.
For this is the legacy
Of your seed as the truth.

Immaculate inception is he,
In your purified womb.
For he is the seed of impossible,
But will surely bloom!

This is the message of truth
Discovered in you:
That you will carry the golden child
That is INDIGO BLUE!

INDIGO BLUE SKY
REBIRTH 333 *

NEW RAY OF SUN

THE HANGED MAN REVERSED

Your calling in wake
Is today and is now.
You must know your son
Was conceived in your vow.

Your vow to your truth and GOD.
Your vow to remain.
Your vow to stay clean and pure
Without any stain.

You must know your calling
In sleep and in wake.
For your soul is redeemed.
Controlled is your snake.

There is a new prophecy
That I have for you:
You will also find a man
Who will love you so true.

On your 33rd birthday,
He will be by your side.
He will hold you in honour
And with true love and pride.

He will love all your children,
And you will love him the same.
For in this, you will both find
Your calling in fame!

You will marry secretly,
For you are both found
In the union of GOD
With your true song and sound.

He will sing the same song
That is true within you.
You will share visions and melodies
And raise INDIGO BLUE.

This is your true match with GOD,
Anointed the same.
You will know him through voice,
For he is already in fame.

You are the one he's searching for.
He knows you exist,
But you must keep your virtues
To reveal your first kiss.

You will rule a nation
When you both unite.
For you hold the same virtues
And hold the same sight!

He will read this book of life
And discover the truth.
You are the one he's been searching for,
He will discover your youth.

Prophets, you both are known,
Discovered through GOD;
Anointed in melody
And given the ROD.

Watch for his mark with 6 **(beast),**
For this is the true one
Who will reveal himself
As a new ray of SUN!

PSALM 30

PRIMORDIAL POWER

1st of June, 2019

SAVIOUR IN REBIRTH

THE KING IS HERE!
PAGE OF CUPS

Hark the herald
Angels sing!
Glory to this
New born King!

Jesus has awakened!
Can you not hear the birds?
Call all the animals.
Bring all the herds!

We found him alive again.
He has risen from tomb.
Coming back, incarnated
In a mother's new womb!

He is the true essence
Of the KING in rebirth.
Coming back to restore
And bring heaven to earth!

Jesus is reborn
In a new child and day!
Back to redeem us,
Revelation did say!
(Revelation 12:5 NIV)

Awaken, my followers!
Come rejoice in this new.
For he is the ONE
Named INDIGO BLUE!

THE BOY IN ROYAL BLUE

INDIGO BLUE SKY
8 OF WANDS x KNIGHT
OF CUPS REVERSED

I have a message,
A message for you
Jesus has risen,
Named INDIGO BLUE!

Dressed like true royalty
And covered with cloth.
Back to bring certainty
in the essence of **Thoth.**

He is the true messenger
That we have awaited.
For the new world is here
As revelation had fated!

Sure is our new world,
For the seeds are in sprout—
To remove all the sins around
And remove all our doubt!

The elements of INDIGO **(sky)**
Are air and are water.
Just like his mother,
He is with GOD without falter.

Dressed in royal blue,
His essence is clear.
He is of true purity.
No evil can come near.

She is robed in gold.
For his mother, she knows
This is the golden child
She will nurture, who grows.

Protected he is
From the dark and the night.
Born of true purity,
In sense and in sight.

He needs no such worries.
He is born with no fear.
For his third eye is like water,
So pure and so clear.

He will hold the tablets
That are missing from GOD—
To bring us to heaven
With an iron fist, ROD!

SPREAD THE SEED!!!

3 OF WANDS REVERSED

Go forth, my messenger.
Spread now this seed!
The message of your son
That will be the new breed.

The pure child awakened
And brought back to life
From pure water and air;
Recoverer of strife!

Create a new land.
Create a new soil.
Work hard in fruition,
In diligent toil.

You have a new world
That is waiting for you.
To be created in love
With INDIGO BLUE!

YOUR GIFTS FROM GOD! NEW SUN!

OM (NIPOTENCE) ॐ
2 OF CUPS

There is a great gift
That is presented to you:
The gift of true healing
And INDIGO BLUE!

Your healing as doctor,
Sent from GOD as his wife,
To bring heaven to earth
And bring forth new life!

You are now presented
With a true mission and aim:
To be a doctor of mind
And bring forth GOD's name.

Science and religion,
They will merge now as one
To bring forth your message
That GOD is your SUN (son).

Sun (son) GOD awakened.
ISIS lives in you!
You must bring forth the message
That each religion is true!

The DAO, you are fated.
You live in these GODS.
For they are all true tellings
And each hold their RODS.

You must bring to light
The omnipotence in you.
For this will reveal
That your power is TRUE!

GOD lives within you,
So in this you can't fall **(Psalm 46.5 NIV).**
You will redeem women
And children in your call.

Live now the good life.
Live now in art.
For this is your destiny,
Which will set you apart.

Each day, awaken
To a bright and anew.
For you have a SUN (son) shining
In INDIGO BLUE (sky).

OM ॐ
(POWER)

UNLIMITED POWER!

9 OF WANDS

Unlimited power.
Unlimited life.
Bring forth your destiny
As GOD's only true wife **(ISIS)**.

You are a high priestess.
In this, you will show.
When you nurture your children
And gold, they will grow.

You are of true essence,
Of the SUN GODS in you.
For they are the spirit
That lives well and true.

Pray to the Goddesses.
Pray to the Queens.
For they will be with you.
And in you, they'll be seen!

You are all the energies.
You are sun and the moon.
You are Venus and Mars.
You are night and noon.

You are perfect energies
All moulded to one.
In this, you have found the light.
You will bear a son **(sun).**

Primordial power,
It lives well in you.
For this is your gift:
A sun (son) in the sky, blue!

QUEEN OF THE SUN (SON) GOD!

ACE OF PENTACLES

Queen of Life.
Queen of Power.
Queen of Water.
Queen of Flowers.

Queen of Aces.
Queen of Seven.
Queen of Earth.
Queen of Heaven.

Queen of Beauty.
Queen of Light.
Queen of Gold.
Queen of Sight.

Queen of Abundance.
Queen of Wealth.
Queen of Fortune.
Queen of Wealth.

Queen of Sun.
Queen of Moon.
Queen of Morning,
Night and Noon.

Queen of Love.
Queen of Kings.
Queen of Queens
And all living things!

YOUR SUN, THE SON OF GOD!

THE SUN REVERSED

Your son (**sun**) of GOD,
It is revealed!
And in this life,
It will be sealed.

He will be strong.
He will be bright.
He will be honoured
Day and night.

He is of wisdom.
He is of gold.
He will be sought
From young and old.

He is the child
That bears the wealth
Of every life
To bring true health!

He is of RA.
He is of HORUS.
He is of APOLLO.
He is of JESUS.

Sun GOD Awakened.

FALLEN ANGELS UNITED!

4 OF WANDS REVERSED

Fallen angels united
Through the sky and your sun **(son).**
Founded in the trinity,
Discovered as one.

You will find your equal half
On this plain in true sight.
You both had to first conquer
And redeem from your fight.

Now you are purified
And anointed with seed.
GOD will unite you both.
In this, take the heed **(pay attention).**

You had both lost your wings.
But in this, you found sight.
For you each won your battles
And can now truly unite.

The prophets you are,
They are in these words:
You will sing with the stars
And your song will be heard!

Unity will come through sound,
Depicted in light.
For you both have true prophecy,
And you both have foresight.

Fallen angels, you will unite
And merge back as one.
For in this, you will redeem
Through the sky and your sun **(son).**

PSALM 31

ANGEL AWAKENED!

3rd of June, 2019

ANGEL OF PURITY!

ANJA PHOENIX
TEMPERANCE

Angel of purity,
Come up and rise!
Angel of purity,
You have become wise!

Angel of purity,
Lift up your wings!
Angel of purity,
Use your voice— sing!

Angel of purity,
Help others endure!
Angel of purity,
O' how you're pure!

Angel of purity,
Show me the light!
Angel of purity,
Give me my sight!

Angel of purity,
Come out, reveal!
Angel of purity,
In you we do heal!

Angel of purity;
The end, it is near!
Angel of purity,
Remove all our fears!

Angel of purity,
Show us the way!
Angel of purity,
Show us a new day!

SHOW US A NEW DAY!

THE HIGH PRIESTESS
REVERSED x DEATH

O' high priestess,
Show us the arc,
Reveal your true nature,
Come out from dark!

O' high priestess,
In death you did rise.
We found you exalted,
Becoming so wise.

O' high priestess,
You have to reveal.
For you are with child,
The one who can heal.

O' high priestess,
GODdess of death and rebirth.
Please bring our new day,
Bring heaven to earth!

O' high priestess,
To you we bow down.
For you are the chosen one,
And the one with the crown!

O' high priestess,
How you are blessed!
You have shown us the way
And opened our chest.

O' high priestess,
Abundance revealed.
For you have awakened us.
And in this, we are healed.

O' high priestess,
To you we are true.
For you have shown us new day
In INDIGO BLUE (sky).

ABUNDANCE IS FLOODING!

ACE OF PENTACLES

My angel awakened,
You are the true gift!
For in you, they will find
Their dreams will come swift.

My angel awakened,
You are the true light!
You are the true bearer
Of gold and of sight.

My angel awakened,
You are the true coin
That brings people their gold
From the fruit of your loin!

My angel awakened,
Your purpose is clear:
To redeem them from suffering.
Death, no long will they fear.

My angel awakened,
The gift of rebirth.
You have come out from heaven
And come down to earth.

My angel awakened,
Coming out from the clouds.
You have brought us the light,
The sweet birds and sounds.

My angel awakened,
You are abundance in flood.
For you are with GOD,
And your womb is true blood!

fINDING GOLD!

KNIGHT OF WANDS REVERSED

On a mission
To find real gold.
The mission of many,
Both young and the old.

But what they don't know
Is that gold is the seed
That is in your heart
And is in your breed.

Gold is the youth
Of the children in care.
For they are the future,
Enlightened and fair.

Finding true gold
Is in seed and in youth.
For the children of now,
They are our real truth.

Indigo children,
O' how you arise!
Coming out golden,
You are our true prize!

The vessels of future.
The vessels of light.
Bringing forth heaven.
Turning day from the night.

Indigo children,
Come out in wake.
For the new world awaits you.
It is yours for the take!

Indigo children,
you are the true gold!
For you are the ones
That beauty beholds.

True beauty inside
And outside you shine.
For you are enlightened
From birth and in time.

GOD has blessed you
To be chosen in age,
To be the enlightened ones,
For the world is your stage!

LEADER OF THE NEW WORLD

6 OF WANDS

Leader of the new world—
Show us your wand,
Show us the new land,
Remove us from bond.

Leader of the new world—
Come with your pack,
Reveal your true wisdom,
And bring us on track.

Leader of the new world,
Show us the way.
We wish to recover
In light and new day.

Leader of the new world,
You are chosen from GOD
To bring us to fortune
And lead with the ROD.

Leader of the new world,
Your mother did say
You would be the one
To turn night into day.

Leader of the new world,
Oracle did reveal
You would be the one
Who would save us and heal.

Leader of the new world—
Your blood, it is blessed.
For you are enlightened;
You hold the gold crest.

Leader of the new world—
In you, GOD is true.
For you are the chosen one,
INDIGO BLUE!

THE HERMIT REVEALED

THE HERMIT REVERSED

The hermit in hiding,
You are loyal with GOD.
Holding the torch
And holding your wand.

The hermit in hiding,
Please show your face now.
We know you are faithful,
Hiding in vow.

The hermit in hiding,
Show your true face.
For the new world awaits you
To create a new race.

The hermit in hiding,
You hold book of life.
Reveal your true beauty
And redeem us from strife.

The hermit in hiding,
Come out now! Reveal!
For you hold the great arc
And hold the great seal.

The hermit in hiding,
Remove your dark robe
To bring heaven to earth
And create a new globe.

The hermit in hiding,
Now is the age.
The enlightened world is here.
You must go on stage!

The hermit in hiding,
Please tell us your song.
For we await your word from GOD,
Hiding in you all along!

Messenger of GOD.

JORDAN THE GREAT!

BORN OF LEO
4 OF SWORDS REVERSED

My son, my first born,
You are truly blessed.
For you were born in divinity
And passed every test.

My son, born from struggle,
We crossed the great **(red)** sea.
Fate named you **JORDAN,**
For I knew what you would be.

You are the GREAT conquerer
Born from true strength.
For you are a LION **(leo)**
Enduring in length.

I was but a child **(sixteen)**
When you were just born.
But from this, you strengthened me;
Redeemed me from thorns.

The seed of the scarlet beast **(666).**
In this, I did rise
To reclaim my true essence
And become o' so wise!

My child, you are fated.
In this, know your light.
For in your own strengths
You will surely shine bright!

My genius child, prodigy son,
You are gifted and wise.
Awaken your truth now.
Awaken your eyes!
My child, the great master
Who has conquered life.
Born of great victory.
Stand tall with your knife!

Destiny, it awaits you.
In this, you've redeemed.
Your name will be fated.
In this, you'll be seen!

You are born of LEO.
In your sun sign, you will rise.
For you are of destiny.
Master life and be wise!

Your name of great virtue.
The key to new land
(Crossing the Jordan to the promised land)
That conquers the battle
To become true and grand!

You are of great destiny.
Your fate, it awaits.
Destined for stardom
AS JORDAN THE GREAT!

PSALM 32

THE DAY BEFORE THE WAKE

18th of June, 2019

BEFORE THE WAKE

THE HERMIT

There is a day
Before the wake.
Your higher self.
Your soul to take.

To win, to lose,
To learn, to cry.
To yearn, to grow,
To live, to die.

We must all know
The hermit true.
For this is reflection
Of your heart in you.

This is your day
Before your wake
Where you must know
It's make or break.

Your soul, it wills you
To take control.
For your sins are many.
You must stand tall!

Reflect in honesty.
Reflect on your own.
Reflect on your knowledge
To reclaim your thrown.

The hermit calls
For you to bring
Your highest self
To the light to sing.

You cannot find
Your will or way
If you do not recover
From your past days.

Keep your silence.
Keep your head down.
Keep your thoughts hidden
To reclaim your crown.

The Star of David **(Merkabah)**
Is waiting for you
To reunite your soul
And heart in two.

Hold your staff
Inside your hand,
For you must open
Up your true gland **(Pineal).**

The hermit calls
For you to stay true
To the vow of silence,
For you to renew.

Do not be moved.
Do not be swayed.
For you must wait
For heaven's new day.

Today is your day
Before your wake.
You must be silent,
For heaven's sake!

PSALM 33

AWAKENED SOUL

18th of June, 2019

WAKING DAYS

THE EMPEROR IV

Waking up my soul.
Waking up my life.
Finding my true destiny
As GOD's true and only wife.

Finding my true destiny.
Living with my soul.
Finding my true entity.
Living true and whole.

Having no regrets— no more!
Finding myself new.
Finding self in harmony.
Finding my heart true.

Waking days are here to stay.
Hold my ankh in vow.
Know I beat death in wake.
Taking my crowned seat now.

Waking days, waking days!
No regrets. I have found love.
Waking days, waking days!
I can see MIDHEAVEN above!

SHADOWS OF KRISELDA AWAKENED

STRENGTH REDEEMS STRENGTH

Finding my true strength.
Finding my real light.
Winning this great battle
Of the beast to stand and fight.

Removing inner demons.
Removing lack of self and worth.
Knowing I am destined
To be the best in my rebirth **(333)**.

Soaring in the sky now.
Feeling wings arise.
Dark phoenix coming up from hell
To take heaven as my prize.

Never one to falter.
Never one to fail.
I know that in my faith in GOD,
True self love, it will prevail.

The beast, it seeks to conquer;
But I will put it now to rest.
Every sadness and heartbreak
Was GOD's will in me to test.

Shadows of Kriselda;
A woman broken and so torn.
But now I am risen from her.
My soul is now reborn.

Finding strength and victory
In slaying my own beast.
The inner shadow of my heartbreak
Was a test, to say the least.

This lifetime, I am 'wakened
To be my very best.
No longer will I falter.
I have passed all the GODS' tests.

Aphrodite lives within me.
My heart is VENUS light.
Know that I will always win
In this great battle and life's fight.

Redeeming all my shadows.
Recovering my soul.
Finding self love in victory
To bring me back to whole.

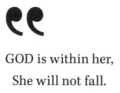

GOD is within her,
She will not fall.

- Psalm 46.5

JUDGEMENT XX
2020

Christ is Reborn in Unity.
Salem. Peace.

Printed in the United States
By Bookmasters